In this highly readable, earthy work of cultural theology, Simmons offers a fascinating and penetrating excursion into the importance of creating local Christian community to forge a kingdom culture. A wonderful antidote to globalist ideology, Simmons uncovers fresh and illuminating insights into the ways in which believers can rebuild a revised Christendom amidst the decay of secular life. Should be on every pastor's shelf.—JOESPH BOOT, Founder, Ezra Institute

When the foundations are destroyed, we must rebuild them locally. Ray Simmons reveals the Biblical blueprints needed for finishing the foundations and then erecting godly orders in small counties and provinces. Imagine: Comprehensive, local, practical, fruitful and covenantal Christianity, lived out within a manageable jurisdiction, with Christians leading, guiding and governing the culture. Ray proves that this is attainable in the 21st century, and why we can begin building with optimism.—GEOFFREY BOTKIN, President, The Atlantic Society for the Study of Culture

Ray Simmons' *The Confessional County* is a must read for today's American Evangelicals. The idea of local civil magistrates confessing Christ and His law might sound foreign to Evangelicals' ears, but that would not be because it isn't Biblical, but because of the contemporary, de facto, pietism and pluralism rampant in the Church. With the world falling to new levels of cultural degradation that we didn't expect in our lifetimes, it is time for Evangelicals to ask themselves if some of the traditions handed down to them were mere traditions of men; and that seemingly "new" voices (*local Christendom*) are whispers of Scripture's solutions to our sin-broken world. I have been an advocate of working toward a confessing county for many years now. However, Ray corrected a key flaw in my assumptions -- a confessional county is not an *End*, but rather a *Way*. To remove land curses and receive select blessings we must understand and live out the message of *The Confessional County*. Through intentional Christian settlements, Ray provides the argument, the vision, and the strategic blueprint to *build*, rather than merely reform, local Christian civilization; a local Christendom.—JASON DIFFNER, Author, *Families in Covenant Succession*

The doctrine of the present mediato
earth, over all the nations, and over

D1246515

6:15; Rev. 19:6) leads to the inescapable conclusion of Confessionalism, i.e., the duty of all mankind to confess Christ publicly as LORD in their personal, family, church, and civil institutions and governments (Phil. 2:9-11; Ps. 2:10-12). The National Reform Association proclaimed that duty to America and carried the banner of National Confessionalism to the States, and applied it to the amendment of the United States Constitution, for over 150 years beginning in 1864. Now, Raymond Simmons, in his book, *The Confessional County*, carries on that noble testimony of the Lordship of Jesus Christ and applies the doctrine of National Confessionalism to, what is perhaps, the foundational unit of American civil government, the local County. This is a book for our times, and it sketches a vision, a strategy, and blueprints for bringing a County under the Lordship of Christ. The book is filled with excellent teaching on such things as land curses, Christ's mediatorial reign, confessionalism, God's law, Christian culture, establishing Christian settlements, and the interposition of lesser magistrates. I recommend this book to all who love and honor the crown rights of King Jesus. –**WILLIAM O. EINWHECTER**, former Vice President of the National Reform Association and Editor of *The Christian Statesman* (1996 – 2007).

The Bible says of David's Mighty Men that they had "understanding of the times, to know what Israel ought to do." Ray Simmons, in this carefully written book, not only identifies the problems with our modern American culture, but he takes the next step by showing us what we "ought to do."—**JOHN HUFFMAN**, Pastor

I highly recommend that Christians read *The Confessional County*, by Raymond Simmons. Even if you are not called by God to move to a county where the principles and strategies of this book can be implemented, the success of this vision should be of great interest to every believer. This book has stirred my blood, given me hope, and made me want to support this effort from afar. Indeed, it is my prayer that as God blesses one county, that others will become jealous of the blessings that flow from God's throne, and county after county will be stirred up by the Holy Spirit to do likewise. God has given a clear plan for how a defiled land can be cleansed at the county level long before it is cleansed at the national level. The time is right for a book like this. May the Lord give it a broad reading and an eager reception.—**PHILLIP KAYSER**, President, Biblical Blueprints

When's the last time you read a book on this subject? Every Christian should read Abraham Kuiper's book, "Lectures on Calvinism," and then immediately read Simmons' book to learn how to implement and correct Kuiper's vision. Simmons' book is delightful to read and compelling because it is based solidly on the whole word of God; it is reader-friendly and it is enthusiastically optimistic concerning the kingdom of Christ. This book tells us how to rebuild Christendom beginning at the local level. His premise maintains that the most effective way to accomplish this rebuilding task in America must begin at the county level. Rebuilding Christendom nationally is impossible without local social confessionalism. My favorite paragraph in this book is the last paragraph in which Simmons refers to the French Calvinists of the 16th century, the Huguenots. He believes that they are a more important study for those of us in 21st century America who are concerned about the shift in our culture from its Christian base than even the English Puritans because "the Hugenots lived as an oppressed nation within a nation."—**JOSEPH MORECRAFT**, Pastor and Author, *Authentic Christianity*

An easy read that flows logically. Mr. Simmons presents a compelling case for the need for the nation and culture explicitly to confess Christ, and gives practical steps, from the beginning, on how to start at a local level. This is the "Covenanter Vision." Highly recommended.—**PHILLIP POCRAS**, Minister, Reformed Presbyterian Church (RPCNA)

Ray Simmons has captured the essence of what it means to advance the Crown Rights of King Jesus and His Kingdom's rule. In a time when only action will suffice, Simmons gives concrete strategies and tactics so that the serious, action oriented, Christian may rescue Christendom from the onslaught of autonomous secular humanism and its tyrannical stranglehold upon Western Civilization, and the entire global order. —**PAUL MICHAEL RAYMOND**, Dean, The New Geneva Christian Leadership Academy

This book is a timely and needed piece of literature for a nation that is suffering the consequences of its rebellion against the Lord. The "Oblique" Simmons writes about is necessary in this hour. May men have ears to hear. As new societies are established from the ashes secularism and statism—this book is indispensable to their structure. Simmons handed us a gold mine!—**MATTHEW TREWHELLA**, Author, *The Doctrine of the Lesser Magistrates*

When the foundations are destroyed, we must rebuild them locally. Ray Simmons reveals the Biblical blueprints needed for finishing the foundations and then erecting godly orders in small counties and provinces. Imagine: Comprehensive, local, practical, fruitful and covenantal Christianity, lived out within a manageable jurisdiction, with Christians leading, guiding and governing the culture. Ray proves that this is attainable in the 21st century, and why we can begin building with optimism.—**GEOFFREY BOTKIN,** President, The Atlantic Society for the Study of Culture

Ray Simmons' *The Confessional County* is a must read for today's American Evangelicals. The idea of local civil magistrates confessing Christ and His law might sound foreign to Evangelicals' ears, but that would not be because it isn't Biblical, but because of the contemporary, de facto, pietism and pluralism rampant in the Church. With the world falling to new levels of cultural degradation that we didn't expect in our lifetimes, it is time for Evangelicals to ask themselves if some of the traditions handed down to them were mere traditions of men; and that seemingly "new" voices (*local Christendom*) are whispers of Scripture's solutions to our sin-broken world. I have been an advocate of working toward a confessing county for many years now. However, Ray corrected a key flaw in my assumptions -- a confessional county is not an *End*, but rather a *Way*. To remove land curses and receive select blessings we must understand and live out the message of *The Confessional County*. Through intentional Christian settlements, Ray provides the argument, the vision, and the strategic blueprint to *build*, rather than merely reform, local Christian civilization; a local Christendom.—**JASON DIFFNER,** Author, *Families in Covenant Succession*

The doctrine of the present mediatorial reign of Jesus Christ over all the earth, over all the nations, and over all peoples (Matt. 28:18-20; 1 Tim. 6:15; Rev. 19:6) leads to the inescapable conclusion of Confessionalism, i.e., the duty of all mankind to confess Christ publicly as LORD in their personal, family, church, and civil institutions and governments (Phil. 2:9-11; Ps. 2:10-12). The National Reform Association proclaimed that duty to America and carried the banner of National Confessionalism to the States, and applied it to the amendment of the United States Constitution, for over 150 years beginning in 1864. Now, Raymond Simmons, in his book, *The Confessional County*, carries on that noble testimony of the Lordship of Jesus Christ and applies the doctrine of

National Confessionalism to, what is perhaps, the foundational unit of American civil government, the local County. This is a book for our times, and it sketches a vision, a strategy, and blueprints for bringing a County under the Lordship of Christ. The book is filled with excellent teaching on such things as land curses, Christ's mediatorial reign, confessionalism, God's law, Christian culture, establishing Christian settlements, and the interposition of lesser magistrates. I recommend this book to all who love and honor the crown rights of King Jesus. −**WILLIAM O. EINWHECTER,** former Vice President of the National Reform Association and Editor of *The Christian Statesman* (1996 − 2007).

The Bible says of David's Mighty Men that they had "understanding of the times, to know what Israel ought to do." Ray Simmons, in this carefully written book, not only identifies the problems with our modern American culture, but he takes the next step by showing us what we "ought to do."—**JOHN HUFFMAN,** Pastor

I highly recommend that Christians read *The Confessional County,* by Raymond Simmons. Even if you are not called by God to move to a county where the principles and strategies of this book can be implemented, the success of this vision should be of great interest to every believer. This book has stirred my blood, given me hope, and made me want to support this effort from afar. Indeed, it is my prayer that as God blesses one county, that others will become jealous of the blessings that flow from God's throne, and county after county will be stirred up by the Holy Spirit to do likewise. God has given a clear plan for how a defiled land can be cleansed at the county level long before it is cleansed at the national level. The time is right for a book like this. May the Lord give it a broad reading and an eager reception.—**PHILLIP KAYSER,** President, Biblical Blueprints

When's the last time you read a book on this subject? Every Christian should read Abraham Kuiper's book, "Lectures on Calvinism," and then immediately read Simmons' book to learn how to implement and correct Kuiper's vision. Simmons' book is delightful to read and compelling because it is based solidly on the whole word of God; it is reader-friendly and it is enthusiastically optimistic concerning the kingdom of Christ. This book tells us how to rebuild Christendom beginning at the local level. His premise maintains that the most effective way to accomplish this rebuilding task in America must begin at the county level. Rebuilding Christendom nationally is impossible without local social confessionalism. My favorite paragraph in this book is the last paragraph in which Simmons refers to the French Calvinists of the 16th century, the Huguenots. He believes that they are a more important study for those of us in 21st century America who are concerned about the shift in our culture from its Christian base than even the English Puritans because "the Hugeunots lived as an oppressed nation within a nation."—JOSEPH MORECRAFT, Pastor and Author, *Authentic Christianity*

An easy read that flows logically. Mr. Simmons presents a compelling case for the need for the nation and culture explicitly to confess Christ, and gives practical steps, from the beginning, on how to start at a local level. This is the "Covenanter Vision." Highly recommended.—PHILLIP POCRAS, Minister, Reformed Presbyterian Church (RPCNA)

Ray Simmons has captured the essence of what it means to advance the Crown Rights of King Jesus and His Kingdom's rule. In a time when only action will suffice, Simmons gives concrete strategies and tactics so that the serious, action oriented, Christian may rescue Christendom from the onslaught of autonomous secular humanism and its tyrannical stranglehold upon Western Civilization, and the entire global order. —PAUL MICHAEL RAYMOND, Dean, The New Geneva Christian Leadership Academy

This book is a timely and needed piece of literature for a nation that is suffering the consequences of its rebellion against the Lord. The "Oblique" Simmons writes about is necessary in this hour. May men have ears to hear. As new societies are established from the ashes secularism and statism—this book is indispensable to their structure. Simmons handed us a gold mine!—MATTHEW TREWHELLA, Author, *The Doctrine of the Lesser Magistrates*

THE CONFESSIONAL COUNTY

Realizing the Kingdom through Local Christendom

To Miriam,
my great encourager

THE CONFESSIONAL COUNTY

REALIZING THE KINGDOM THROUGH LOCAL CHRISTENDOM

RAYMOND SIMMONS

NEW DUNEDIN PRESS

Names: Simmons, Raymond, author.
Title: The Confessional County: Realizing the Kingdom through Local Christendom / Raymond Simmons.
Description: Red Oak: New Dunedin Press, 2021. Includes bibliographical references.
Identifiers: [978-1-5136-8475-8] (print)
[978-1-5136-8476-5] (ebook)

Quotations from the Holy Scriptures are taken from the King James Version.

Printed in the United States of America.

ACKNOWLEDGMENTS

This project was beyond my capability, but the Lord provided help through His Body, the church.

I am so thankful to John Huffman. Pastor Huffman is a diligent student of the Bible and history. He answered every question I asked him and provided many helpful suggestions. When I needed a resource, he knew the book to point me to. His positive approach refreshed my soul.

My own pastor, Phillip Kayser, is a scholar and servant who loves God's Word. His work has helped many apply the Scripture to every area of life. He pours his life into others, and I'm one of those happy recipients.

I appreciate Joe Morecraft, who took the time to encourage me that the confessional county was biblical and worth the effort.

Robert Fugate's work on curses, his understanding of Scottish confessions, and his personal guidance was invaluable.

I'm also thankful to the men who have been fighting the good fight of National Confessionalism. Many thanks to William Edgar, William Einwechter, and Phil Pockras. They took the time to help me understand national confessionalism better. Their work is not in vain in the Lord.

Hannah Dykstra used her amazing gifts to create a beautiful cover. I appreciate her patience with me.

And finally, I thank my own family. All hands were on deck for this project. My wife and all my children prayed and did the things I could not do when I was locked in my study. My daughter Elizabeth has been my excellent executive assistant and more.

CONTENTS

INTRODUCTION

In October of 2020, my wife and I logged into a Zoom meeting hosted by Heritage Defense with about fifty other homeschooling families. The session was about how to legally protect our families in an environment of forced vaccinations. About ten minutes into the meeting, someone asked a question that sparked a flurry of remarks. The question was: "Is it time for us to do the Benedict Option?" The chat in the sidebar lit up. Someone asked, "Where do we go?" Another responded, "We're ready to move."

I turned to my wife and said, "I have to write a book." I was encouraged that people had realized the dire situation Christians in the United States were facing. It seemed these people were willing to take drastic measures, including moving, for their families' future. I was concerned, however, that these families might do it in a fearful and a non-covenantal way.

My answer to the question "Is it time to do the Benedict

Option?" is this: *Yes, it's time, but please don't do it the Benedict Option way.*

The Benedict Option is a book written by Rod Dreher in 2017. It calls for a strategic withdrawal to set up Christian communities. According to Dreher, the culture has gone too far, and it's time to regroup. Dreher recommends we stop wasting energy piling up sandbags to stop the flood. Rather than fighting the current structure, "we should instead work on building communities, institutions, and networks of resistance that can outwit, outlast, and eventually overcome the population."[1] He says it is time for some Christians to build rather than reform, and I agree with him.

I think Dreher gets the current status correct, and that's important. We need to know the strategic landscape. But more important than the current status is our *trajectory*. In a military planning session, *where we are* currently is not as important as *where we are headed*. We can accept a bad SITREP (Situation Report) as long as the Strategic Outlook is good. Any conflict will have some bad SITREPs. But if the briefing officer does not show a path toward victory, the general will fire him and get another briefer the next morning. The trajectory is more important than the current analysis.

Eschatology is trajectory on a grand scale; it's where God is taking this whole thing. And eschatology is in one sense more important than our current laws and cultural practices. If we know where we are going, we can make better decisions today, even in a defiled land. Trajectory (of the eschatology sort) will also affect our motivation. If we see failure on the horizon, our human hearts will not be as courageous as if we see victory. A positive view of our eschatology (particularly in an earthly, tangible sense) increases our level of effort.

However, this positive view can also have a negative effect if we are not careful. We can put things off too far into the future, kicking the can to the next generation because, after all, the conditions are not favorable now. But I think P. Andrew Sandlin is on point. In his most recent book, *Realized Religion,* he writes, "One of the most prominent errors in the history of the church is postponing massive blessings of creation and the gospel to the eternal state."[2]

So trajectory is more important than current status. This leads me to my next point: *structure is more important than trajectory.* This is because *structure determines trajectory.* How a society is built matters greatly. Is it built with a covenantal structure with God? Or is it built upon any one of the many humanist ideas?

Here is my first challenge in this book: I aim to prove that the core problems of our culture are structural. The US slowly developed into a pluralistic state with autonomous laws. But that is the wrong structure. The structure we really need is comprehensive Christianity. We need everything built upon Jesus Christ and His law. Therefore we don't just need a reboot; we need a whole new operating system. The most important structure we need is covenant, and social confessionalism is a way to get that.

What is social confessionalism? Glad you asked. Social confessionalism is the model presented in the Bible where all-of-society comes together and representative heads of family, church, and state confess their societal sins, covenant with God (specifically with our mediating King, Jesus), and commit to following all of His commands. This is how a society taps into God's grace as a society. Now we have a new structure. Now societal sins can be forgiven, land can be healed, and we can go forward—as a society— in blessing.

This sounds great. But almost immediately an objection arises. Most Reformed Christians are not opposed to confessionalism; they just don't think now is the time. They say, "We'll get there someday." There is some solid logic behind this way of thinking. At the end there will be a much greater manifestation of comprehensive Christianity. Nations and societies everywhere will confess Jesus. Yet we seem to have missed the fact that before worldwide conversion, social confessions will happen along the way.

So why do we tend to defer social confessions of Christ until the future? One reason is based on our view of society. Today we see society *atomistically.* We see it in terms of individuals, families, churches, and the civil magistrate.[3] We think God sees it that way too. Of course, God *does* see individuals, families, churches, and magistrates distinctly. The question for us here is this: how does God see all of society?

I think the older understanding was better. The Scottish Covenanters, the Huguenots, the early American settlements, and to some extent Christendom writ large had a better understanding of how God sees society. They believed God saw society in covenantal terms. Because of this view, they were more inclined to see the necessity of a social confession *as a way to start.*

If they were here today, they might use a photography illustration. God doesn't take snapshots of different segments of society and Photoshop them into a collage in post-processing. Rather, in addition to His individual snapshots, God takes a group photo. He has a wide-angle lens in His bag for this purpose. If the group picture is a good one, Christ is seen at the front as the mediating King; then representative heads of the family, church, and civil magistrate are behind. So we have the Ruler in front and His institutional vice-regents standing in supporting ranks. The vice-regents are not perfect: their uniforms are dirty, and they can't really stand still. But Jesus is perfect, and He is pleased (the whole Trinity is pleased) because this rag-tag group just signed up to be a Christian society. They still have a lot of training to do, but at least now they have the right structure.

My second challenge flows from the first: I aim to demonstrate that things such as confessionalism, comprehensive Christianity, and beautiful culture are not just results of the Great Commission; they are integral to the advancement of it. Since we lost the wide-angle view of societies, we also lost the view that the City on a Hill and the Mountain of the Lord are *causal.* God uses them to cause things to happen. Today we seem to miss this. We tend to overlook the fact that a City on a Hill will cause *heathen* nations to be jealous, which means this city exists in the midst of heathens. I will make the argument that an all-of-society approach is needed for the City on a Hill to do its thing. Church, family, and magistrate are all vital components of this city. A community of the church and families (without the civil magistrate) isn't a city. The comprehensive city has all of Jesus' institutions, and it is distinct from culture. Eschatologically, the temporal City on a Hill exists on the pathway to the eternal City coming down out of heaven.[4]

My third challenge is where the rubber meets the road:

I endeavor to show my readers that the low-population rural county is worth moving to. There are different ways of implementing social confessionalism, but I see no better-suited environment than the rural county in the US. Today's rural counties offer significant opportunity and stability, especially with remote work and logistics extending to essentially every rural location (thank you, Mr. Bezos). We will see how the rural county allows us to build culture rather than reform it. Most importantly, we will see there is an opportunity to get out of national curses at the county level.

Like Dreher, I believe we are at a point where some people should execute strategic withdrawal. I just want us to do it from a covenantal perspective. I do not believe this strategic withdrawal violates Jesus' desire not to take us out of the world. Until moon-colonization goes live, we're not going very far.

Before we start, please allow me to address some concerns you may have:

1. I am not promoting the social gospel. Salvation does not come through society and programs.

2. This is no Utopia. It will not be perfect. I cover what Utopia really is and how to avoid utopian approaches in chapter thirteen.

3. I am not saying everyone should do this. Short of a direct command to flee, Christians can please God right where they are.

4. This is not a hunker strategy. We'll discuss some defensive elements, ones that may prove very beneficial (necessary) to our families, but we'll mostly focus on an offensive flanking attack to be executed as the Lord

enables. I think there are wise ways to do this without causing legal problems.

5. I am not saying that the wide-angle view of society is the only way God sees us. I am saying, however, that this is missing in our understanding today.

We can characterize our goal as "Local Christendom." As Douglas Wilson and Douglas Jones write in *Angels in the Architecture*, it will be the "Second Christendom." The Second Christendom will be better than the first because it is more thoroughly biblical. This Christendom will be composed of imperfect mini societies covenanted with a perfect God. Its beginnings will be small. Our confessions and commitments may be unofficial at first. We may not be able to completely start over. We may not be able to get all the way to biblical law, but confessing that we are committed to Christ and His commands is a step in the right direction. It sets a structure for success.

Lastly, I want to pass on a warm-hearted warning from a dear pastor friend of mine. When he read an advanced copy of this book, he told me that the contents are biblical, *but there was something missing*. The thing that was missing was the love of Jesus and the love of all of the Trinity. He told me that if I don't emphasize our love of God and our love of each other, all our efforts will be sounding brass. I re-wrote some sections based on this wise counsel.

With God's blessings, the old doctrines in this book will have a new impact. The hope is to help other counties, our states, our nation, and the world confess Christ. It will be one of the many ways, but an important one, to realize the Kingdom.

I pray this book will be an enjoyable and profitable read.

—Ray

> Through God we shall do valiantly: for he it is that shall tread down our enemies. (Psalm 60:12)

THE OBLIQUE

I hope, so soon as practicable, to attack.[1]
STONEWALL JACKSON

Chancellorsville, 1863. To those who know the battle, you know what I am talking about when I say "Chancellorsville." I am talking about a risky but well-founded strategy that combines maneuver, surprise, and economy of force. This isn't a frontal-attack strategy.

At Chancellorsville, it wasn't so much that Lieutenant General Stonewall Jackson brought new ideas. It was that he put the ideas into practice with energy and with prayer. Jackson built upon Frederick the Great and, to some extent, Napoleon. Frederick the Great's introduction of the "oblique" is considered game changing in military history.[2] His army was smaller, but his tactics were better. With the enemy pinned down in the front, Frederick would maintain a reserve echelon to exploit success or cover a retreat and dispatch a select contingent to attack his enemy's weakest flank.

Whereas Frederick codified the doctrine, Jackson was the one who really put feet to it. His "foot cavalry" (marching thirty miles a day was standard) brought the oblique to life. Jackson showed us that maneuver *in and of itself* is a weapon. Adding swift maneuver to the oblique was very effective. It still is. The Special Forces were birthed from this idea and maintain a crucial part in Joint Strategy today.

But I doubt Frederick and Napoleon were Jackson's only mentors. Since Stonewall was a fastidious Bible student, he probably knew every detail of Joshua's second attack on Ai (the successful one) by memory. This was the one where he sent 30,000 chosen men, "mighty men of valor," away by night to position themselves in the rear of Ai. Joshua knew his enemy (like Jackson knew the Federalist, Major General Hooker). He knew Ai was prideful of their last victory and would let down their guard. The ruse worked perfectly. When the men of Ai ran out to pursue Joshua's feigned retreat, this rear force took the city.

Joshua was consistent in his idea of a proactive, fast attack. He often did this after a long march upon an unsuspecting enemy. He attacked the Southern allied kings of Canaan "suddenly" (Josh. 10:9), and he did the same with the Northern kings (Josh. 11:7). The Northern kings were probably still in garrison as happy campers when Joshua attacked them.

Strategy is often about speed, but it is also often about it cousin, timing. Both Jackson and Lee knew this was their time at Chancellorsville. R. L. Dabney writes, "That Hooker must be attacked, and that speedily, was clear to the judgments of both."[3] It turned out to be Jackson's best battle—and his last. He was able to get well around the enemy's rear, marching twenty miles, including three miles through thick brush. Stonewall constantly waved his hand and said, "Press forward." His energy and strategic mind had enabled the defeat of 125,000 with only 45,000 men (Jeb Stuart also deserves much of the credit).

Stratagems from General and Special Revelation

We should not shy away from secular writers on strategy. Stonewall Jackson didn't. He was steeped in Sun Tzu, the Chinese general from 500 BC, and Clausewitz, the Prussian military theorist who was nine years old when the mob stormed the Bastille in the French Revolution. Stonewall was learning from strategists whose life and campaigns spanned 2300 years. There is an amazing consistency to the elements of strategy.

It seems that the elements of strategy are built into creation, similar to the laws of logic. Greg Bahnsen, whose battle as a Christian apologist was different from Jackson's (but no less important), did not hesitate to use Aristotelian logic (after adding a good dose of biblical refinement, of course). He slew the ideas of the atheist Gordon Stein in "The Great Debate" in 1985. Like Jackson and Bahnsen, we should be willing to use principles of strategy discovered (not developed) by the secularists. If for no other reason, we should read them because our enemies do. Even Karl Marx was a student of Clausewitz's strategy. He wrote, "Among other things I am now reading Clausewitz' *On War*. A strange way of philosophizing but very good on his subject."4

As useful as secularist ideas of strategies are, the Bible is our all-sufficient war book. Paul Michael Raymond writes, "all strategies and tactics must have a moral foundation based in Scripture if they are to have any legitimacy and lasting impact."[5] That is our goal here, to see where Scripture provides not only a way out of curses—not only a way to survive—but a way to secure generational blessings and ultimately to have the whole world recognize Christ and His law.

The Bible does have strategy. Even the creation account in Genesis gives the ways (methods), means (resources), and ends (results) of this six-day campaign to bring everything from nothing. The "ways" were God speaking things into existence. There was only one "means," God Himself; otherwise, He would not have created *ex nihilo*.[6] The "end" was a creation so good that God was willing to kick back and enjoy it.

But God was not done with strategy after creation. Since the Fall, the Bible is in one sense a strategic campaign of God reversing the curse and bruising the head of Satan. God's Grand Strategy is the redemption of His elect and all creation through Jesus Christ. "And, having made peace through the blood of his cross, by him to reconcile all things unto himself; by him, I say, whether they be things in earth, or things in heaven" (Col. 1:20). Let's not miss the "all things" and the "earth" shown here to be part of God's campaign.

Local Christendom, the Oblique

"Local Christendom" is a sub-strategy that supports God's Grand Strategy of redemption. It is a sub-strategy we haven't used in quite some time. Most likely, we have not used it because we have been under the construct of the great-nation state and a long march toward centralization. But those trends are reversing, and localism is on the rise.

The etymology of "Christendom" means Christ has *dom*inion in time and space, here on earth. Depending who you ask, Christendom can be time-bound as starting with Constantine and ending with Napoleon. Constantine confessed Christ; Napoleon ignored him. The thing about Christendom is that it was never fully Reformed. Theology waxed and waned on the purity scale, but Christendom ended before it went full-scale Protestant and Reformed. The next Christendom will have better theology to build upon because, by His grace, we are coming to the unity of the faith (Eph. 4:13).

This Second Christendom will likely be more localized at first. For our purposes, when we say "local" Christendom, we are talking about a society small enough to allow for accountability and ownership. The ones who rule there are the ones who live there. You can go to the county commissioner's meeting every week, and you will know which commissioner wants to raise taxes. When there is a parade in town, you will know what kind of parade it is going to be. You will know what is going to be "paraded." When the town theatre schedules a séance by a satanist for Halloween, the locals say, "Not in my town!" and it doesn't happen.

This is the type of society we see in the Bible, one where we have access to our rulers, one where we actually sit down and eat with them (Prov. 23:1), one where they are held accountable by families and the church.

By local Christendom, we also mean a society large enough to have all the basic functions of society. It has its own government, businesses, and newspaper. It has its own culture. The rural county is a good expression of this because, while it is small, it is fully functional. It may not have everything you want, but it will have everything you need. This leads to a certain level of local sufficiency, identity, and "self-rule," which we intend to make "Christ-rule." The doctrine of social confessionalism, when combined with the doctrine of the lesser magistrate, seems to be a good fit to reverse course and get under God's blessings.

I am proposing that local Christendom is a *"way"* of Kingdom advancement and that it is possible to achieve in our own lifetime or at least our children's lifetime. The confessional county is our oblique maneuver. Rather than fighting the culture head-on, we march around it. This is an attack on Satan by plugging in officially, covenantally, *geophysically* to Christ *before* the United States is wholly Christianized. We seize the initiative and get out from under land curses. We do this by confessing Jesus as Lord of the county and asking forgiveness. That breaks the curse and brings the high ground of covenantal blessings from which we can press the attack further to other counties and the state, nation, and world.

Maxims and stratagems underlie the philosophy of this book. Maxims are the principles, the doctrine behind *The Confessional County.* Stratagems give the top-level approach. These are codified in Appendix A.

How do we implement this strategy for local Christendom? I recommend we do it one small county at a time. A deliberately chosen rural county with a small population is well-suited for this strategy. People would have to move (like you read about). Moving to a deliberately chosen rural county secures a very good fighting position, in my estimate.

Could you employ this strategy in a town like Manhattan Kansas, population 54,604, for example? Yes, but in that case, you are more into reforming rather than building. In my research, any county above about 10,000 people will have established structures and an established culture. (See chapter eleven on localism for more on this idea.) Reforming is still a good approach, but it is different from building. Naturally, some of the principles do overlap. The doctrine of social confessionalism can be applied anywhere there is a civilization, but what I am presenting is a focused strategy that really calls for a specific environment.

You could perhaps apply the principles of this book if you lived in (or migrated to) a small country. The states in the US are about the size and population of a typical country, so you could reach a national confession there about the same time as a state confession here (remember, Jesus told us to count the cost of building, Luke 14:28). I think American families should have their passports ready in case an urgent need or a new opportunity appears. However, overall, the US legal construct is good, and the Spirit does seem to be moving among Christian home-schooling families here. So right now, my target is the rural county in the US.

I believe today's situation calls for an oblique maneuver, and the confessional county is an option. Notice I said *an option.* While I am very confident in this strategy, I am not saying everyone should do this. Not everyone went with Stonewall; not every one of Joshua's troops went to the backside of Ai.

If this all sounds novel, if it sounds too much like the

latest-book-on-Christian-culture-engagement, I want to say a few things. There will be some "new" things, but by "new," I mean developments or refinements since the mid-1800s. The doctrines of national confessionalism, comprehensive Christianity, theonomy, reconstruction, interposition, and nullification are not new, but they have been further developed or at least brought to the forefront *after* the Christian colonization of the 1600s and 1700s had largely ended. We have some new war plans on the shelf.

What this strategy does is flip the timing on its head. We try to get to local confessionalism—county confessionalism—*within decades* rather than centuries or millenniums. This is local Christendom.

A small number of Christians finding success can melt the heart of a pagan nation. I think we are well-postured for a second wave of Christian settlements, colonizing rural America and confessing Christ locally. This is our oblique.

2

SITUATION REPORT

I t's over. That was Rod Dreher's assessment in *The
Benedict Option*. I think he was right, and I think we
needed to hear that. Dreher writes, "There are people alive
today who may live to see the effective death of Christianity within our civilization."[1] Christianity will survive,
but based on current trends, it may not survive in the
United States.

Dreher says we lost the culture war, and we lost the
public square. We could pick many examples, but *Obergefell*
naturally floats to the top. Sodomy has become our officially recognized and celebrated policy. And just to make
sure there is no place in America where you can follow
what the Bible says about marriage between husband and
wife, the federal court system overreached and made it "the
law of the land" (even though the Supreme Court does not
make law).

Perhaps the biggest change was not the new pro-
sodomy law but the change in the public's conscience.
According to the American Values survey in October of

2020, 70% of Americans now support marriage between sodomites (though they use a different term).[2] The *Obergefell* ruling is very telling of where we are, not just because of the fact the unthinkable has become "law," but because God allowed this type of thinking.[3] It means something even worse than homosexuality becoming legal; it means God has given us up. According to Romans chapter 1, God did not give us up because of socially-accepted homosexuality; rather, socially-accepted homosexuality *is because God gave us up* (Rom. 1:21, 24, 28). Being given up by God is about as bad as it can possibly get. Once God withdraws His hand of blessing, it really is over (Isa. 43:13). There is no future unless we somehow get "non-given up" as a society.

It has gotten even worse in the three years since Dreher's book. He wrote his book before Black Lives Matter, Cancel Culture, Woke, rioting, intersectionality, critical race theory, or any other word that puts a fresh face on Marxism. Before November 2020, we used to think election fraud was for the Sandinistas, but now even common trust and respect for the law are in short supply.

In 2020, Dreher wrote a second book, *Live Not by Lies*. He wrote this one during "Corona" times. In this book, he shows the US has the same indications that other countries had before their communist revolutions. I think he gives a fair assessment. His sources, people who lived through communist revolutions, said they knew they had lost their freedom when they lost their outside voice. Whenever they started to speak softly—*privately*—about what they believed, the ship was going down. It was just a matter of time. What we see today is that Christians in the US are losing their outside voice. Today we speak with a *new inside voice*, end-to-end encryption and Facebook alternatives.

Don't get me wrong; end-to-end encryption is great and we should use it. But the fact that we need it indicates we have lost our outside voice.

What was particularly helpful in this second book from Dreher was the idea of "soft totalitarianism." Soft totalitarianism is what we experience today. It is not the totalitarianism of old that comes from Russian czars with cigar and vodka breath and impressive mustaches. Our totalitarianism is more refined—more subtle—but probably more destructive. Today it comes from corporations and the media who can turn the heart and mind of a nation to the point where all common sense is gone. When corporations adopted LGBTQ "rights" as policy, it was only a matter of time before we accepted it as a societal norm and law. The corporations knew what they were doing, and it all worked out just as planned.

Core Problem #1: Autonomy

I think it's even worse than Dreher presents. It's worse because our societal roots are deep and pulling water from the wrong source. For example, Marxism is a problem, but it is not the core problem. The core problem (the root) is the philosophy of *human autonomy* behind Marxism, the idea that man can develop his own laws and ethics apart from the Bible. Marxism is but one branch of human autonomy. You get rid of Marxism—but not human autonomy—and there will be another problem on your hands just as dangerous. Modernism was Abraham Kuyper's concern, and that is another form of human autonomy. Much of this thinking goes back to Greek philosophy, a philosophy not according to Christ. They planted the wrong seeds. Gary DeMar writes, "The School of Athens typifies man's love for knowledge independent of God and His Word."[4]

I think the Reformed perspective is helpful here. We are either ruled by God's law, which is perfect and endures forever, or we are ruled by man's law, which seeks to establish its own righteousness and hasn't gotten it right yet.[5] Jesus was not happy with man's law as exhibited in the Pharisee's tradition. Jesus was not opposed to law—He did not come to abolish it, after all—but He was opposed to laws made without recognizing and aligning with the laws of Scripture. Laws not rooted in the ethical system of the Pentateuch were "the tradition of men" according to Jesus (Matt. 15:3; Mark 7:8).

By God's grace, God's law had a good run as the controlling influence over Western culture. Matthew Trewhella points out, "For nearly 1500 years throughout Western Civilization the objective standard was the rule of law."[6] William Blackstone, whose writing was very influential on early American politics, shows how we used to think of the law of God. He writes, "It is binding over all the globe in all countries, and at all times."[7]

Not only have we lost the principle that our laws are supposed to reflect God's laws, but we have also lost the idea that *the law*—not a person—*is king*. In other words, in a covenanted society, we are to bind ourselves to obey the laws, not a particular person. Today's politics is more about power and personality and what "the people want" than about the law. The media's coverage of the 2020 election did not focus on the law but on what people were saying. Unhitching from God's law, and even from the concept of law itself as we saw in 2020, brings us closer to everyone-doing-what-is-right-in-his-own-eyes, which is autonomy, which is our number one societal problem.

Core Problem #2: Pluralism

Another problem Dreher mentions is the lack of righteousness. This certainly is a problem, but I think it's more of a fruit than a root. The root of an unrighteous society is *pluralism.* Pluralism is the idea that mutual worldviews and life systems can exist side by side. Our Puritan settlers definitely opposed pluralism,[8] and it was still somewhat guarded against by our Continental Congress. One of the original grievances the Continental Congress of 1774 enumerated against Parliament was "for establishing the Roman Catholic religion in the province of Quebec."[9] Not only were they opposed to pluralism in their town; they didn't even want it on their new continent.

I would categorize pluralism into four levels.

1. *Level 1 Pluralism.* A belief that the official, public practice of different religions should be allowed, but Christianity is recognized as the only true religion. This is also known as "Principled Pluralism."
2. *Level 2 Pluralism.* A belief that pluralism is a strength and should be encouraged. "We can learn from all religions."
3. *Level 3 Pluralism.* A belief that no single religion has all the truth.
4. *Level 4 Pluralism.* A belief that Christianity must be kept private. Because Christianity claims to

have exclusive truth and universal ethics, it is
disqualified as a public religion. This is what I
call *hyper-pluralism.*

All of these levels are prohibited in the Bible. Many
verses disallow pluralism, and we will go over many of
them later, but for now we will just use the First
Commandment, "Thou shalt have no other gods before
me" (Ex. 20:3).[10] This does not mean that God gets first
place at the table of gods, that He is the first of many. It
means that there are no other gods allowed at the table *at
all.* Since He is omnipresent and especially since He owns
the entire planet (Ps. 24:1), He is unwilling to share His
glory. In times past pluralism was overlooked, but not
anymore. "And the times of this ignorance God winked at;
but now commandeth all men every where to repent" (Acts
17:30).

There is a natural development from Level 1 to Level 4.
We have cruised the road from principled pluralism to
hyper-pluralism, which means that today everything is
accepted and celebrated except biblical Christianity.

Aaron Renn, author of the *Masculinist* newsletter,
breaks up the Christian's relationship with society into
three periods, and I think he shows the progression of
pluralism (although he may not characterize it that way).
His analysis shows that in less than thirty years, Christians
have gone from having a positive position in the world to a
negative position.[11] Here are his categories:

1. *Positive World (Pre-1994).* To be seen as a religious
   person and one who exemplifies traditional
   Christian norms is a social positive. Christianity

is a status enhancer. In some cases, failure to
embrace those norms hurt you.

2. *Neutral World (1994-2014)*. Christianity is seen as
a socially neutral attribute. It no longer has a
dominant status in society, but to be seen as a
religious person is not a knock either. It's more
like a personal affectation or hobby. Traditional
norms of behavior retain residual force.

3. *Negative World (2014-present)*. In this world, being
a Christian is a social negative, especially in
high-status positions. Christianity in many ways
is seen as undermining the social good.
Traditional norms are expressly repudiated.

In the "Positive" and "Neutral" worlds, Christians
permitted pluralism, but pluralism now prohibits Christianity. (Again, I'm don't think Renn would characterize
pluralism as the problem—that is my own analysis. But I
think his construct is very insightful).

Pluralism is really polytheism because every societal
issue is a religious issue, and every religion has its god.[12] The
type of state-sponsored pluralism we have today is essentially rulers who "take counsel together, against the LORD
and against his anointed" (Ps. 2:2). This is the opposite of
kissing the Son, and it puts us on the wrong side of Psalm 2.

In his book *The Myth of Political Polytheism*, Gary North
shows us the folly of thinking we can ever hope to receive
societal blessings in a pluralistic society.[13] North pulls no
punches. God did not cancel our obligation to His ethical
standards for the civil magistrate in the New Testament,
and those standards do not allow for pluralism. Unfortu-
nately, the founders of our country were greatly influenced

by "Enlightenment" thinking, and while not pluralistic themselves, they opened the door nice and wide for us. I think David Carson said it best when writing of pluralism in *God and Politics:* "We live in a state that is constitutionally committed to this position."[14] Maybe the founders were not intentionally promoting pluralism, but they allowed for it, and that was all that was needed.[15]

I believe Dreher's *Benedict Option* gives us a very accurate analysis. Dreher is right: we lost the culture war. Someone with a national audience of Christians needed to say this. But an in-depth strategic analysis needs to deal with the mechanisms by which we lost and fuel behind those mechanisms. Our societal problems are structural in nature: human autonomy and pluralism. These are the engines behind secularism, Marxism, statism, institutional infanticide, state-sponsored sodomy, and all the rest. One law, one Lord—accessed by covenantal connection—could have prevented this (Lev. 24:22).

Listen to what the Reverend David Scott wrote in 1841:

> The distinguishing characteristics of the present age, is hostility to the doctrine of Christ's dominion over the nations; and, the practice consequent upon this, of refusing to apply the scriptures as the universal rule in civil as well as in religious matters.[16]

That is our distinguishing characteristic today, in full bloom. It is clear that we have given up God and (more seriously) have been given up by Him as a nation. It is time to admit it, and it is time to recognize the reasons for it.

One may ask, "How did we get here?" I think the simplest answer is that we did not preach the gospel in the way Jesus told us. We forgot the requirement to teach all the commandments that Christ has given us. Those commandments do not allow for autonomous laws or pluralism. We will look at ways to address our structural problems by starting over to the maximum extent. But first, we must discuss land curses.

3

LAND CURSES

Son of man, when the land sinneth against me by
trespassing grievously, then will I stretch out mine hand
upon it, and will break the staff of the bread thereof, and
will send famine upon it, and will cut off man and beast
from it.

EZEKIEL 14:13

A land curse is a curse on a society. It is tied to the
physical earth, but the concept of a land curse has a
broader meaning that includes the geographical boundaries and the society that lives there. The curses of
Deuteronomy 28:15-68 and Leviticus 26:14-39 are land
curses, for example. They come in many forms. There is
the general land curse, which means that the society associated with that land is not receiving help from God
(although He may still be preserving them, Lev. 26:45).
Then there are specific land curses, from Deuteronomy 28

for example. Here are some of those curses: business failure (v. 16); few children, poor crops, few animal offspring[1] (v. 18); difficulty in all tasks (v. 19); national disasters, confusion[2] (v. 20); pandemics[3] (v. 21); fevers, burning, scorching winds, war, mildew (v. 22); drought (vv. 23-24); defeat (v. 25); death (v. 26); skin diseases, scurvy (v. 27); insanity, blindness, numbness of heart (v. 28); lack of prosperity, oppression and robbery (v. 29); marital infidelity (v. 30); loss of resources (v. 31); and more. I think you get the idea. These curses on a society operate twenty-four hours a day and seven days a week (v. 19). The important thing to see is that these are curses on society, not individuals (Deut. 28:9-11).

We are swimming in land curses today. We have to be if we believe the Bible's ethics and that God is consistent and just. It may be that we are so insulated from fluctuations in crop production and economics we do not realize it. Or it may be that we have become numb to the sin that's everywhere present. But the Bible says we're guilty, and the data shows it is happening.

Famine, which in broad terms means economic hardship, is a land curse (Ezek. 14:13). Here's an interesting chart from the Congressional Budget Office that shows our current and projected economic state. The Pandemic of 2020, which has all the makings of a land curse, put a jetpack on the back of our national debt. Our debt to GDP ratio is at wartime levels and will likely continue its ascent.[4]

Federal Debt Held by the Public, 1900 to 2050

Percentage of Gross Domestic Product

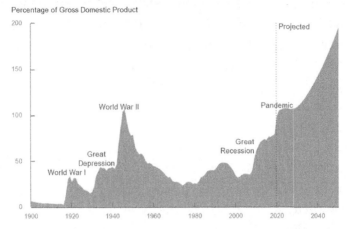

But what got us into this Pandemic? Only God knows for sure which one of our many sins caused it; however, the national discussion right before the Pandemic was whether or not children should choose their own gender. Nationally, we seem to be of the mindset that gender selection is a good thing, something to be extolled. Isaiah would not approve: "Woe unto them that decree unrighteous decrees" (Isa. 10:1).

Do Land Curses Apply Today?

A natural question arises: "Do the land curses of the Bible apply today?" The answer is yes, they do, and for many reasons. First, Adam's curse was a land curse over the whole earth, and it still has residual power. Adam heard those dreadful words directly from God, "cursed is the ground for thy sake" (Gen. 3:17). Every broken promise, stolen car, or wrecked marriage has its root there. And land curses are not just for farmers. The "land" is essentially the earth and everything we need from the earth to live. God can punish everyone with a land curse because everyone depends upon the land. An agrarian friend of mine told me the earth's entire population depends upon six inches of topsoil.

Thankfully, since the great sea change of Christ's crosswork, we have a way out of Adam's worldwide land curse. We are reconciled to God through Christ, who crushed the head of the serpent. Creation is getting better, but it is still groaning and will remain groaning until it is completely renovated (Rom. 8:22). As the basis of all land curses, Adam's land curse is still with us but in decreasing measure.

The second reason land curses apply today is that they were not just for Israel. The principle behind the curses, the moral law, applies to all of God's created order. Leviticus 18 shows us that even non-Israelite nations were under land curses for their disobedience. They specifically violated God's law, and they defiled the land. In other words, every nation that broke God's law was guilty of local land curses.[5] We read in Leviticus 18:24-25:

> Defile not ye yourselves in any of these things: for in all these the nations are defiled which I cast out before you: and the land is defiled: therefore I do visit the iniquity thereof upon it, and the land itself vomiteth out her inhabitants.

So every nation is defiled (and their land is defiled) if they are in disobedience to God.

The third reason land curses apply today is that the Great Commission carries with it God's law, which includes the blessings and the curses.[6] "Teaching them to observe all things whatsoever I have commanded you" means teaching the law. And it is not just individuals but nations who have to obey Him. Since Christ came, and since the Gentiles are grafted into the church, the responsibility of nations outside of Israel has actually *increased.* Jesus now owns the whole world, specifically the heathen nations (Ps. 2:8). Just as Joshua (a type of Christ) conquered Canaan (a type of the world) and brought the law in all its measure, so does Christ today.[7] Land curses are with us today because all nations are under obligation to Christ's law.

The fourth reason is taken directly from Jesus' teaching. In addition to His famous overall statement that not one jot or tittle would pass away (Matt. 5:17-18), Jesus showed us that even the specific penalties of the case law[8] are still in effect (Matt. 15:4).[9] Since Jesus saw the law as a whole (Matt. 7:12), we have to conclude that the blessings and curses of Deuteronomy 27 and 28 apply today. Therefore it should come as no surprise to us when we see Jesus upholding the curse construct. In Matthew 10:14-15, Jesus showed us that whatever house or city does not receive the gospel, that house or city is cursed.

In sum, we know land curses still apply today because Adam's curse is still here, because curses have always been levied on disobedient nations (not just Israel), because the Great Commission carries God's ethics to the world, and because Jesus specifically declared that houses and cities can be cursed in the new covenant.

Is the United States under Land Curses?

Let's bring this a little closer to home. If land curses still apply today, what are the specific violations that cause them? We will look at some sins that cause land curses and see how we as a nation are doing.

1. LAND CURSES DUE TO KILLING THE INNOCENT.

> So ye shall not pollute the land wherein ye are: for blood it defileth the land: and the land cannot be cleansed of the blood that is shed therein, but by the blood of him that shed it. Defile not therefore the land which ye shall inhabit, wherein I dwell: for I the LORD dwell among the children of Israel. (Numbers 35:33-34)[10]

These verses tell us two important things. First, killing the innocent defiles the land. God is the creator of life, and the only lawful way to take life away is by His command. Killing the innocent breaks His law-covenant and defiles the land. Notice the phrase "wherein ye are." This land curse is not for the whole world—it is localized. We are *geospatially* living in either defiled or undefiled land.

These verses also tell us there is only one way for the land to be cleansed. The murderer must be executed. As Rushdoony says in his *Theology of the Land* series, "The land has no atonement apart from the enforcement of God's law."[11] God owns the land. Jesus is King. God has always required blood for blood; otherwise the land is defiled (Num. 35:33).

So, how are we doing? We are under a land curse

because of (1) shedding innocent blood and (2) not cleansing the land. The facts are condemning. In 2018, the estimated number of murders in the nation was 16,214.[12] According to the Numbers passage above, every one of these murderers must be executed for the land to be cleansed. Can you guess how many convicted murderers were executed in 2018? Twenty-five—in the whole nation.[13] That means that 0.1% of all convicted murderers in the US receive the punishment God requires.

The statistics are worse when we consider the murder of the unborn. The approximate number of abortions in 2018 was 875,658.[14] That means that the ratio of killing the unborn to that of biblical punishment is .0029%. But it must be 100% to avoid land curses. We are doubly guilty here: first, we killed many innocent babies, and second, we did not punish those who killed them. The land, according to the Bible, is defiled with blood.

The "good news" is that the US is the only remaining country in the West with the death penalty; however, President Biden has pledged to eliminate it. He is just following the cultural trend here. The trend is away from what the Bible requires on capital punishment. BBC writes, "A November 2019 Gallup poll found that 60% of Americans supported life in prison over the death penalty for the first time since the survey began more than 30 years ago."[15]

2. LAND CURSES DUE TO SEXUAL IMMORALITY.

Leviticus 18 lays out sins of sexual immorality. Incest, adultery, bestiality, and homosexuality are all condemned side by side. The "things" mentioned in the verses from Leviticus we read earlier are primarily these sexual sins. Notice what these "things" do:

> Defile not ye yourselves in any of these things: for in all
> these the nations are defiled which I cast out before you:
> and the land is defiled: therefore I do visit the iniquity
> thereof upon it, and the land itself vomiteth out her
> inhabitants. (Leviticus 18:24–25)

Any one of those sexual sins would defile the land. I will point out again that this land curse was localized to the nations practicing these wicked things. Those nations were localized in Canaan. When Joshua's troops marched into the land, the land was already defiled. But the Israelites would inherit a cleansed land because they would destroy the nations of Canaan that defiled the land.

It is clear that even if the US started with an undefiled land, we have now defiled it by allowing sodomy to go unpunished. We are at a point now where we celebrate the very things that cause the land to be cursed.

3. LAND CURSES DUE TO SABBATH-BREAKING.

It used to be that the only stores open on the Lord's Day were those of necessity. The Westminster Confession lays out the historical Reformed view that was the basis for this practice. We are to rest, all the day, from worldly employ-ments and recreations and to spend the time in public and private worship and in duties of necessity and mercy.[16] The lack of Sabbath observance was one of the main reasons why the Pilgrims left Leyden, Holland. They knew the Lord would not bless a land that continues to break the Sabbath.[17]

The Sabbath is something that has to be enforced by the civil magistrate. Nehemiah gave a stern reminder to the civil leaders of the returned exiles.[18] He reminded them that one of the reasons they were taken to Babylon in the first place was because they did not practice and enforce the Sabbath.

> Then I contended with the nobles of Judah, and said unto them, What evil thing is this that ye do, and profane the sabbath day? Did not your fathers thus, and did not our God bring all this evil upon us, and upon this city? yet ye bring more wrath upon Israel by profaning the sabbath. (Nehemiah 13:17-18)

In our country, civil leaders have not enforced the Sabbath for hundreds of years. We have pushed aside the Fourth Commandment, that God does not allow work by us or by our servants (employees) on His day.

4. LAND CURSES DUE TO IDOLATRY.

Leviticus 26 tells us that idolatry causes land curses.[19] The Heidelberg Catechism number 95 gives a helpful definition of idolatry:

> Idolatry is to conceive or have something else in which to place our trust instead of, or besides, the one true God who has revealed Himself in His Word.

Idolatry is also defined in terms of actual, physical idols, the "worship of an idol or a deity represented by an idol, usually as an image."[20] The Buddhist statues that I see when I drive to church are such items. Is there any doubt idolatry is ubiquitous in our country? Not only do we have idolatry in practice; we have idolatry institutionalized.[21] In Exodus 34, God makes His ethic quite clear: there will be no other religions practiced publicly among God's people; even the altars, images, and groves have to be cut down (Ex. 34:11-14).[22]

The reason for God's prohibition of false religions is simple; He is jealous, "For thou shalt worship no other god: for the LORD, whose name is Jealous, is a jealous God" (Ex. 34:14).

Land Curses, Societal and Geographical

Land curses, even in the new covenant, are bound by societal and geographical lines. In Jesus' passage below, He presents the concept of shaking the dust off your feet against a particular house or city.

> And whosoever shall not receive you, nor hear your words, when ye *depart out of that house or city*, shake off the dust of your feet. Verily I say unto you, It shall be more tolerable for the land of Sodom and Gomorrha in the day of judgment, than for *that city*. (Matthew 10:14-15, emphasis added)

Calvin's commentary says: "To shake off the dust from the feet was probably a custom then prevalent in Judea, as a sign of execration; and was intended to declare that the inhabitants of the place were so polluted, that the very ground on which they trod was infected."[23] Shaking off the dust was to declare a land curse. Paul and Barnabas actually did shake the dust off their feet, just like Jesus said to do, when the Jews and chief men of Antioch rejected them (Acts 13:51).

We can learn many things from this "dusting-off." Here

we see that the curse was *societal*. When Jesus used the word "whosoever," He referred to a collective society, in this case a house[24] or a city, but the principle applies to any society. It is a distinct set of people. Also, the passage shows us that it is *geographical* because it is a place you can "depart" from. Lastly (and this is important for the confessional county strategy), the cursed house or city is evaluated separately from the whole nation. Cities are judged separately. It will be worse for "that city" than for Sodom and Gomorrah and, by logical extension, the whole nation.

In other words, land curses are not necessarily national. Some areas within nations are worse than others. Therefore we can also say that *some areas are better than others*. If a city can be cursed, it can also be blessed. And this is true even if the city exists under a higher civil authority.[25]

The message Jesus was conveying is that some cities are not going to receive the gospel, and they will be cursed. The flipside of this coin also must be true then: some cities will accept the gospel and be blessed. Whether or not a society is blessed or cursed depends on its response to the gospel and obedience to God's commands.

There are other biblical examples of societal, geographic curses. While whole nations are sometimes cursed, God often curses specific cities and towns and the land immediately surrounding them, as He did with Sodom and Gomorrah (Gen. 18:20-21; 19:13, 25). In Deuteronomy 13:12-18, God calls for the destruction of a city given to idolatry, which includes any established religion besides what God has authorized.[26]

Isaiah discussed Damascus as a geographically cursed place: "The burden of Damascus. Behold, Damascus is taken away from being a city, and it shall be a ruinous heap" (Isa. 17:1). Job 24:18 says a murderer will cause a geographic curse: "their portion is cursed in the earth." There are also prophecies against the cities of Tyre and Sidon. And most important for us, Jesus shows that geographic towns are cursed *in the new covenant.*

> Then began he to upbraid the cities wherein most of his mighty works were done, because they repented not: Woe unto thee, Chorazin! woe unto thee, Bethsaida! for if the mighty works, which were done in you, had been done in Tyre and Sidon, they would have repented long ago in sackcloth and ashes. (Matthew 11:20-21)

Jesus began to upbraid (or denounce) the cities because they *as a city* did not repent. This is a good example of God having a wide-angle view as well as an individual view of society.

Since land curses come to societies and their areas, someone may ask, "Can I move out into the country and get out of land curses?" I see this mindset often—perhaps you have too—that people are going to "get out of Dodge" and hunker down somewhere safer. There is support in the Bible for fleeing to avoid impending judgment (Luke 21:21); however, the countryside is not an entity unto itself. It is not free from covenantal obligations. Deuteronomy 28:16 says, "Cursed shalt thou be in the city, and cursed shalt thou be in the field."[27] God still considers the surrounding countryside to be tied to its parent city (Deut. 21:1-3, Jer. 19:10), to its civil society and magistrate. This is why it's important to find a location where you can have a righteous county seat. Just moving into the country surrounding a cursed city, for example, will not get your family out of the curse of that city according to the Bible.[28]

The Biggest Problem with Land Curses

Can there be any doubt that our country, once blessed, is now under God's curse? This is bad, but it's actually not the biggest problem. The biggest problem with a land curse is that you can't go forward as a society until the curse is removed. I think we have failed to see this crucial point. We can still have successful evangelism and pure worship in the midst of a cursed land, but the societal curse has to be removed before societal progress (such as righteous laws) can be made.

Joshua is a clear example. His forces could not win a battle no matter how sincere their efforts because they were under a curse.

> Therefore the children of Israel could not stand before their enemies, but turned their backs before their enemies, because they were accursed: neither will I be with you any more, except ye destroy the accursed from among you. (Joshua 7:12)

It wasn't until the Israelites found and destroyed Achan and all his family and possessions that they were under blessings again. One family with one unapproved garment and some silver and gold had to be removed for the nation to move forward. After that, they were unstoppable (Joshua 8).

Haggai is another good example. The people in the book of Haggai were charged to rebuild the temple, yet they were not progressing because they were under a land curse and did not even know it. They saw the decrease of production (a land curse) but did not know why. Thankfully for them, the Lord spoke through Haggai: "Consider your ways" (Hag. 1:7). God told them this curse had come because they were seeking their own prosperity apart from their religious duties (v. 9). It was their self-serving disobedience that caused the drought (land curse) upon the land and "upon men, and upon cattle, and upon all the labour of the hands" (v. 11). Only after Zerubbabel (the governor) and Joshua (the high priest) and *all the people* came together and feared God did the Lord say, "I am with you" (v. 13). Only then did the Lord prosper the work of their hands.

What these passages show, and what we need to grasp, is how God deals with societies collectively. A society will have a mixture of good and evil, but it is the overall covenant-establishing and covenant-keeping that makes the difference. This is nowhere more clearly presented than in Deuteronomy 27-30, and that is why this passage is a crucial text for the confessional county. We will discuss this more later, but for now, I want us to see the binary path God sets before nations. After laying out all the reasons for blessings and curses, the passage culminates with a choice of two paths going disparate ways:

> I call heaven and earth to record this day against you, that
> I have set before you life and death, blessing and cursing:
> therefore choose life, that both thou and thy seed may
> live. (Deuteronomy 30:19)

Remember, this section of Scripture is dealing with a society (Deut. 28:9-11). It seems the condition of any given society is binary: they are blessed, or they are cursed. Certainly there are degrees, but the overall condition is determined by covenantal faithfulness.

Assyria was on the wrong side of this coin. That was the nation that was cursed of God in Isaiah chapter 14, and

Isaiah says that curse could not be disannulled (Isa. 14:27). Only God can remove a curse He has levied.

It's also important to note that this blessing or cursing status is based upon *current* actions or obedience. "For this commandment which I command thee this day, it is not hidden from thee, neither is it far off" (Deut. 30:11). In other words, the requirements of Deuteronomy 27-30 are not *goals for the future but requirements for today*. This is why I'm advocating we find a way to keep covenant very soon. We are currently under blessing or curses because of our current actions (and our covenantal status—but more on that later). Being under a curse by definition means that you cannot go forward with the blessing of God.

God's People under National Curses

We don't want to take this too far and say there is no protection for Christians in a cursed land. As we have seen, the Bible holds societies guilty for societal sins, and even God's people suffer in that situation. However, the Lord still marks out His people and can still bless them. Jeremiah 17 provides a case in point. The sin of Judah is written with the point of a diamond upon their heart (v. 1). As a nation, they have idolatry, and God will cause them to serve their enemies. In verse 5, however, the Lord changes the perspective from national to personal. Verse 5 says, "Cursed be the *man* that trusteth in man, and maketh flesh his arm." After showing that a particular man can be cursed, Jeremiah gives the other side of the coin and shows a particular man can be blessed:

Blessed is the man that trusteth in the LORD, and whose hope the LORD is. For he shall be as a tree planted by the waters, and that spreadeth out her roots by the river, and shall not see when heat cometh, but her leaf shall be green; and shall not be careful in the year of drought, neither shall cease from yielding fruit. (Jeremiah 17:7-8)

So God still holds out blessings for faithful families and churches even in a cursed society.[29] As God's people in the new covenant, we have a greater promise of God's presence.[30] He set His seal of the Holy Spirit on us (Eph. 1:13) and promised He would never leave us (Matt. 28:20). We will still get caught up in the societal punishment for land curses, but even in that time, God will not forsake us (Ps. 91).[31] The point I am making is that a cursed land is a big problem for us. We can still call out and find individual and family blessings, but societal sins stick around for generations unless we employ a societal solution.

The Bible is clear that land curses are not relegated to the old covenant, and it is clear that the ethics that place societies under curses have not changed. When we look at our nation, there can be no doubt we are on the wrong side of this blessings/curses coin.

Here are the two most important things to remember:

First, you cannot achieve societal progress while under societal (land) curses.[32] The historical biblical examples of Joshua and Haggai show this. God will not forsake His people even under a land curse, but we should not expect societal progress.

Second, God dispenses curses or blessings in a geographical and societal way. If God will curse a local society for bad, surely He will bless that local society for good. As we will see later with Nehemiah's example, even if there is a higher civil government under curses, God still recognizes inferior, small societies as distinct and able to be forgiven of land curses.

In 1648, the Scottish Covenanters recognized that their society was corporately guilty. Knowing that societal sins require societal confession, they bonded together as "Noblemen, Barons, Gentlemen, Burgesses, Ministers of the Gospel, and Commons of all sorts," and wrote a document to confess their public sins. It was titled, "A Solemn Acknowledgment of Publick Sin and Breaches of the Covenant." They acknowledged the source of their land's pestilence, famine, and war. They said, "we cannot but look upon these things as from the Lord."[33] And neither can we.

4

CHRIST'S MEDIATORIAL REIGN

The kingdoms of this world are become the kingdoms of
our Lord, and of his Christ; and he shall reign for ever and
ever.

REVELATION 11:15

In 2012, the US military made a change. We called it the
"pivot." We realized that Russia was no longer our
main concern, and we pivoted to the Pacific theatre.
China's hegemony had become more important and more
threatening. We changed the strategic allocation of forces
because the situation had changed.

The biggest pivot in world history happened with the
cross-work of Jesus Christ. His death, burial, resurrection,
ascension, and coronation changed everything. He became
King of the world. The question, however, is whether or
not we've grasped the full measure of this. We've gotten
our minds around the resurrection when He declared

victory over death. But have we gotten ahold of the truth of Jesus' coronation? Do we understand the world has a new societal order?

In some sense, we do. We pivot around Jesus' work chronologically. Our dating system counts down to Christ and up since Christ. In the past, the church worshipped on the last day of the week, looking forward to His rest. Now we worship on the first day as Christ has equipped us to go forward, knowing that He has overcome the world. However, my suspicion is that even though we changed our weekly schedule, society does not consider why. Most Christians today have not grasped the full weight of Jesus' ascension to the right hand of God. But Peter did. Listen to what he preached about Jesus' avant-garde position:

> For David is not ascended into the heavens: but he saith himself, The LORD said unto my Lord, Sit thou on my right hand, Until I make thy foes thy footstool. Therefore let all the house of Israel know assuredly, that God hath made that same Jesus, whom ye have crucified, both Lord and Christ. (Acts 2:34-36)

Here Peter exemplifies the early preaching of the church: Jesus is Christ, and Jesus is Lord. A common misconception today is that Christ gets the Kingdom at the end of time. Actually, it is the opposite. That's when He gives it away, gives it to the Father (1 Cor. 15:24-25). In the meantime, Christ is a *working* King, reigning until He makes His foes His footstool (Ps. 110:1; Acts 2:35). He owns the territory (Matt. 11:27; John 17:2), and He is subduing enemies by the Sword of the Spirit. He is doing this primarily in pockets of geophysical societies (more on this later).

The resurrection gives us great confidence that we have eternal life. It is for the future. But the coronation gives us great confidence that Jesus owns the world today. We should almost have an aloofness to any thoughts that Satan is still in charge. Satan, although still working havoc through demons, is defeated (Jas. 4:7). We read in Hebrews 2:14:

> Forasmuch then as the children are partakers of flesh and blood, he also himself likewise took part of the same; that through death he might destroy him that had the power of death, that is, the devil.

What this means is that our approach to a fallen world comes in Kingdom context. Jesus is at once Lord and Christ. The proclamation of the gospel in the first century was not just about personal salvation; it was also about the kingship of Christ. Herod tried to kill Jesus when he heard He was King of the Jews. Jesus assumes the Davidic throne (Matt. 1:1). His ministry was the ministry of the Kingdom. The prayer He taught us—*The Lord's Prayer*—has the Kingdom at the heart. When asked by Pilate, He did not deny He was King of the world.[1] He could have chosen any theme to end His earthy ministry with, but at the end of Matthew's Gospel, His authority was the theme. William Edgar says that Jesus' all-authority proclamation is "the most important political fact of our time."[2]

Furthermore, Jesus told His followers they would witness to kings *for His sake* (Mark 13:9; Acts 9:15). And it happened. Paul tried hard to convert King Agrippa (Acts 26:28-29). The apostles and later Christians preached *to kings* over and against the kingship of Caesar. This was the "problem" with Christianity. This was the primary reason they suffered so much persecution. It wasn't so much that Christians had to worship Caesar; it was that Caesar had to worship Christ. Edgar writes, "Converted kings have to give up claims to their own divinity and, like every Christian, publicly confess Jesus. Then, like all Christians, they must obey God in their callings on earth. For kings, that means ruling according to the law of God, not according to what merely seems good to them."[3] Edgar explains that the kings didn't like this proposition.

Polycarp, when dragged to the stadium as an old man, refused to swear by Caesar. He asked, "How can I blaspheme my King that has saved me?"[4] According to Polycarp, blasphemy is denying the kingship of Christ. Caesar had no right to claim sovereignty over the world. That was insulting the crown rights of King Jesus. There can be only one sovereign, and that message was an insoluble part of early gospel presentations.[5]

County Implications of Jesus' Kingship

Jesus, as we know, is a prophet, a priest, and a king. A prophet brings the word of God. Jesus is actually truth incarnate, in flesh. You don't get more prophet-like than that. He purifies His people as a priest. But it takes a *king* to win a military battle, to rescue an imprisoned people. William Symington, a Scottish pastor in the early 1800s and author of *Messiah the Prince,* says that Jesus' kingly office is necessary for His gospel work. He must have regal power to secure our redemption.[6] As Isaiah wrote, "For the LORD is our judge, the LORD is our lawgiver, the LORD is our king; he will save us" (Isa. 33:22).

For the confessional county, we are interested in Jesus'

current reign over all institutions, with a special look at the civil magistrate. A. A. Hodge gives us a good sense of what's at issue here:

> If Christ is really king, exercising original and immediate jurisdiction over the state as really as he does over the church, it follows necessarily that the general denial of neglect of his rightful lordship, any prevalent refusal to obey that Bible which is the open law-book of his kingdom, must be followed by political and social as well as moral and religious ruin.[7]

Hodge's words are simple and direct. If we deny that Christ is the rightful Lord of the state as well as the church, our ruin is moral, religious, political and social.

Earthy Christianity

Because Christ came to redeem the world and is reigning now, what we have is an earthy Christianity. Jesus is redeeming all things in earth and in heaven to Himself (Eph. 1:10; Col. 1:20), and we're further along the track than we typically think in the modern church. Eschatology is more realized than we realize, even in the midst of a culture that seems hell-bent on going back to paganism. Isaiah 2:2 says, "And it shall come to pass in the last days, that the mountain of the LORD's house shall be established in the top of the mountains, and shall be exalted above the hills; and all nations shall flow unto it." Calvin comments on this verse: "When he mentions the end or completion of days, let us remember that he is speaking of the kingdom of Christ."[8]

The "last days" are not future but past. They were gradually fading out, starting at 1400 BC and finally expiring in AD 70. We are now in the "New Age."[9] John Gill writes, "wherever the last days are mentioned, the days of the Messiah are intended."[10] Acts 2:17 and Hebrews 1:2 both put the "last days" as the days already attained by the time of the New Testament.

Since we live now in His Kingdom as Isaiah 2 shows us, the "green light" is on for the concept of the LORD's house being established on the mountains and all "nations" running into it. The confessional county (actually *any* society) can become the mountain *today*. However, we should acknowledge that there is some "not yet" in Isaiah chapter 2. Our swords are not plowshares yet (v. 4). We still do have war; the 20th century was a terrible century for warfare. But the thrust of this chapter is that with the Messiah comes the concept of a civilization set apart to follow God's law and compel others to follow that example.

New Heavens and a New Earth

A very important consideration centers around the phrase "a new heavens and a new earth." When does this new heaven and new earth occur? Does it occur in eternity, or does it occur in history? In other words, does it occur after the final resurrection and judgment or before?

The common understanding is that it happens in eternity, after the Great White Throne judgment. That is a correct understanding. The chronological flow from Revelation 20:11 to 21:1 shows that this is in eternity future. Judgment comes first; a new heaven and a new earth come second. But that's not the whole story. Phil Kayser, in his Revelation Sermon series (probably the most extensive research and preaching project on Revelation to date),[11] says that the "new heaven and the new earth" exists in eternity, but it actually *starts in history*. It started with Jesus' incarnation, life, cross-work, resurrection, ascension, and coronation. In other words, we're living in the early stages of the new heaven and the new earth today.

John was not original when he used the phrase "a new heaven and a new earth" when he wrote Revelation. He was pulling from Isaiah 65. This brings up an apparent problem. In Isaiah we see birth and death still happening in the "new earth" (v. 20), but after the final resurrection, there will be no more death (1 Cor. 15:26; Rev. 21:4). In other words, Isaiah clearly points to a new heaven and a new earth that is on this side of the Judgment—in history. That seems to contradict Revelation. So, which is it?

It is both. When we understand biblical gradualism, as Kayser's work points out, the seeming contradiction evaporates. The Kingdom of heaven grows from a mustard seed to a full tree (Luke 13:19). Three measures of leaven eventually, gradually leaven the whole loaf (Luke 13:21). Christ is in the *process* of reconciling all things to Himself, "whether they be things in earth, or things in heaven" (Col. 1:20). He is reigning *until* He has put all things under His feet (1 Cor. 15:25).

Augustine upheld this gradualism. Speaking of the new heaven and the new earth, he said, "For this world will pass away by transmutation, not by absolute destruction." He points to 1 Corinthians 7:31-32[12] to show it is the "fashion of the world that passeth away,"[13] not the world itself.

To use a modern metaphor, *we are living in Narnia, and it has begun to thaw.*

Why is this important for the confessional county? Because it shows that seeking to have as much heaven on earth as possible is not escapist. On the contrary, seeking to keep heaven far off, to keep heaven and earth separate, *is escapist*. That approach allows people to be so heavenly-minded that they're no earthy good, as the quip goes. The Gnostics wanted to keep a healthy distance between history and eternity, between the physical and the spiritual. They would prefer to escape this world rather than deal with it.[14] Speaking of these Gnostic escapists, Kayser writes, "Typically escapists deny a gradual application of redemption and insist instead upon a cataclysmic replacement of everything at one sudden point in history."[15] That makes it more comfortable because rather than getting messy with current, earthy things, we can gently push heaven's ethics into the future. But this is out of line with Jesus' current reign.

The kingship of Christ has gone live, and we haven't "realized" it to the extent we should. The pivot happened at the Cross, and of the *increase* of *His* government there shall be no end.

We are not saying that earth is heaven. There's some now-and-not-yet going on. Hebrews 12 talks about the *now*, "But ye are come unto mount Sion, and unto the city of the living God, the heavenly Jerusalem, and to an innumerable company of angels" (v. 22). Verse 28 says, "Wherefore we are receiving a kingdom which cannot be moved." So Hebrews chapter 12 tells us what we have today. However, the very next chapter talks about the *not yet*. It tells us that we have "no continuing city, but we seek one to come" (13:14).

Putting this all together means that the earth is not a condemned rent house scheduled for the wrecking-ball.

Rather, it is a house that we co-own with Christ, one that we can improve along the way, and one that gets a renovation at the end that is better than any HGTV show ever produced.

Every Christmas, I go see Handel's Messiah. If you have been, you might have wondered why everyone stands at the Hallelujah Chorus. The chorus is based on Revelation 19:6, 11:15, and 19:16. But why do we stand up for this? We stand up (as oral tradition has it) because King George II stood up. Upon hearing these words, he rose to his feet as the most powerful king in the world, responding appropriately to Christ's greater kingship.[16] The chorus goes like this:

> *Hallelujah! for the Lord God Omnipotent reigneth.*
> *The kingdom of this world is become the Kingdom of our Lord, and of His Christ: and He shall reign for ever and ever.*
> *King of kings, Lord of lords.*

King George may not have had everything correct, but he knew who his Boss was. Christendom knew Who was in charge.

Now, imagine a county in which practically everyone goes to hear Handel's Messiah sung on the town square on a cool December evening. Elegant Christmas lights are hung in the stores. The children sport hot chocolate mustaches. Imagine all county commissioners, the state senator who lives there, the judges, pastors, and heads of household gathering around with their families. When the orchestra and choir get to the chorus, everyone stands up from their lawn chairs. *And they actually know why.* They know, and they acknowledge, "The kingdoms of this world are become the kingdoms of our Lord, and of his Christ; and he shall reign for ever and ever."

5

COMPREHENSIVENESS REQUIRED TODAY

Obligation to obey divine law is entire.
REV. DAVID SCOTT, 1841.

In 1898, B. B. Warfield invited Abraham Kuyper to speak at Princeton for the Stone Lecture series. Dr. Kuyper said something surprising at this event. He said that Calvinism had never fully blossomed; it had never reached the stage of a "life-system." Paganism, Islamism, and Romanism had reached the stage of life-systems, but not Calvinism. In the late 1700s and early 1800s when it was time for Calvinism to take center stage, the stage was stolen by modernism, the daughter of the French Revolution.[1] Modernism effectively jettisoned the church from political and social life. Ironically, it was France's expunging of the Roman church that had prevented Calvinism from attaining life-system status in the Western world.[2] Calvinism was collateral damage in the revolt against all things church.

It seems strange that Kuyper would say Calvinism never really had its day. After all, what about Geneva? What about early Puritan America? Were not they Calvinistic? What he meant was that Calvinism had not developed into a comprehensive way of life that enveloped everything the way (say) Romanism had. Pockets of Calvinism existed, but Calvinism as doctrine *and practice* had not so permeated the world as to be a system. Calvinism had greatly influenced governmental documents, but there had not been a sustained group of nations under Calvinism comprehensively.

Kuyper is very institutional in his thinking. He may be a bit too institutional,[3] but he brought to light a biblical doctrine that has dramatically helped our understanding of Christ's Kingdom. With his famous "not one square inch"[4] statement, Kuyper showed us that Jesus abominates the idea that any part of life is not under His reign.

Comprehensive Christianity is Christianity proper. Christ ordained three social institutions—the family, the church, and the state—and these three institutions are complementary and interdependent. The church brings the gracious Word of God that transforms souls (Rom. 10:14). It maintains righteousness by church discipline (1 Cor. 5:4-7). It counsels the state on ethics (Mark 6:18). The state punishes evil (including heresies) and rewards good (Rom. 13:4), protecting the church and family. It calls for synods so that the church can inform society and rulers on right and wrong (2 Chr. 19:8).[5] Isaiah is speaking of the new covenant people of God when he says the civil magistrate must protect the church: "And kings shall be thy nursing fathers" (Isa. 49:23). The family and the church provide people well-suited to the civil magistrate, able to rule well (2 Sam. 23:3; 1 Tim. 3:7). Make no bones about it: Christianity was designed to operate as an interconnected system.

One of our biggest problems is that the civil magistrate is not fulfilling its part in the Kingdom. The civil magistrate, indicative of the broader culture, does not (in the main) come from Bible-saturated families and churches that faithfully preach the whole counsel of God. This notable shortfall has led us to focus on the family and the church in the short term. We categorize the civil magistrate as a long-term project and "focus" on church and family today.

The problem with this approach is that we don't have comprehensiveness. We are trying to fly an airplane with a three-bladed propeller where one blade is significantly shorter than the other two. Ask any pilot. If a propeller breaks off in flight, the procedure is to shut down the engine because the vibration will make the plane unflyable. You have to land. Like an airplane, society doesn't fly with only two of three institutions properly attached to the power Source.

I met a man at a pastor's conference that came from a good family and a solid church. All his children were homeschooled. All were faithful, except one. That one was a recently-adopted teenager from another country. She filed a complaint of child abuse because she disdained the house rules. All the man's children, including the faithful ones, were subsequently taken away from him and his wife while they awaited trial. While his children were in the custody of the state, they were strip-searched so "investigators" could check for abuse. They found none.

At the conference, this man was in tears. His family had

been under persecution, and his customers had dwindled down to only those people who knew him well. The situation he experienced was characterized by a medium-bladed church, long-bladed family, and a short-bladed civil magistrate. The checks and balances that God put in place were not existent. The church should have interposed, and the civil magistrate should have listened to the church and at least required multiple witnesses. They should have known God did not give CPS the right to do what they did. Families are hurt when things are out of balance.

Elements of Comprehensiveness

There are two essential elements in biblical comprehensiveness, two "alls," if you will: *all-of-the-commands* and *all-of-society*. We see both "alls" side by side in the Bible. Joshua did all that was commanded him (Josh. 11:15), and he took "the whole land" (Josh. 11:23).

The first element, *all-of-the-commands*, shows us the all-inclusive nature of God's law. Joshua is a very relevant example because he is a type of Christ, and the Promised Land is a type of the whole earth. At the very outset, Joshua is given the requirement for success. He has to meditate on the book of the law "that thou mayest observe to do according to all that is written therein" (Josh. 1:8). If the "all" condition fails, the promise of being prosperous and having "good success" is nullified.

Similarly, the initial verse of the blessings-and-cursings section of Deuteronomy says this:

And Moses with the elders of Israel commanded the people, saying, Keep all the commandments which I command you this day. (Deuteronomy 27:1)

God is emphatic that obedience to all the commands is the condition of blessings. He repeated the word "all" multiple times in Deuteronomy's blessings and curses section (Deut. 27:3, 8; 28:1, 15).

The second element, *all-of-society*, comes on the heels of the first. You simply cannot keep the commands if you do not keep them as a comprehensive society. When we look at the social covenanting recorded in the next chapter of Deuteronomy (chapter 29) we see that the whole society stood and committed itself to the law.

The *all-of-society* requirement is also presented indirectly by various commands: *fathers* are to lead according to God's gracious commands and provide for their families (Deut. 6:6-9; Prov. 13:24, 22:6; Eph. 6:4); the *church* is to be a prophetic voice and to be pure (Rom. 1:16; 1 Cor. 1:18); the *civil magistrate* is to rule according to God's Word: "He that ruleth over men must be just, ruling in the fear of God" (2 Sam. 23:3).[6]

I said there were two elements to comprehensiveness, but actually there are three. The third element gets at the heart. All the commandments must be kept "with all thine heart, and with all thy soul" (Deut. 30:10). God wants all our heart. He will not bless external, cold law-keeping that has no love for Him (Isa. 1:11). This is crucial: the comprehensiveness of God cannot be veneer. It has to go deep into the souls of individuals and subsequently infiltrate the culture of a society. As with our individual lives, Christ's grace must shine forth because we cannot follow God corporately unless we are connected to the Vine (John 15:5).

I don't know about you, but sometimes I am reading along in the Bible and find it strange that God inserts a passage about love. I almost think, "Wait a minute, we're talking about very important stuff *to do*. Why are we talking about love all of the sudden?" For example, take Deuteronomy chapter 10. Moses just made the second set of tablets (the replacement ones). God wrote on them. The Creator of the universe *wrote on them!* Moses comes down from the mountain and tells the Israelites to pack up and begin marching. They begin their journey, repositioning to go in and possess the land (v. 11). And God stops it all and says this:

> And now, Israel, what doth the LORD thy God require of thee, but to fear the LORD thy God, to walk in all his ways, and to love him, and to serve the LORD thy God with all thy heart and with all thy soul, (Deuteronomy 10:12)

God continues talking about how He loves them and how they need to circumcise the foreskin of their hearts in order to better love Him back (vv. 15-16). He even tells them to love the fatherless and the widow and the strangers among them (vv. 17-19). We would not naturally be thinking about love at critical times like this. But love is not an afterthought according to God. Love is the prime mover.

I am writing this interlude about love because God may be repositioning us for a big event. And if He is, it may be easy to forget God's love. It may be easy to overlook our brothers in need. But thankfully, the most important commandment of the Bible is also the easiest to remember.

> Jesus said unto him, Thou shalt love the Lord thy God with all thy heart, and with all thy soul, and with all thy mind. This is the first and great commandment. And the second is like unto it, Thou shalt love thy neighbour as thyself. On these two commandments hang all the law and the prophets. (Matthew 22:37–40)

In all of our planning, our evangelizing, our rebuking of bad civil magistrates, our educating our children, and our fighting the ungodly culture—in all of it—we must remember that love of God and love of our neighbor is the reason we do it. Only with love is Christianity truly comprehensive.

Community is Not Enough

Sometimes Christians react to oppressive civil magistrates and decadent culture by pulling back and building "communities." Dreher's *Benedict Option* takes this approach. The idea is that members of the church will take care of each other in times of need. That is good as far as it goes, but the problem is that the civil government is still in charge of civil matters, and resisting an evil government as an *informal community* has not boded well in history.

Ask the Huguenots. They knew that community was not enough. They actively pursued and supported kings that would help them, and they even created their own political arm. William Henry Foote wrote an excellent book on the Huguenots. He writes:

> The name Huguenot . . . is supposed to mean *Confederate,* and was applied to those who leagued together, or confederated, to preserve their civil liberties against the encroachments of the nobles, and the encroachments of the Romish church. [7]

King Navarre and the Bourbon line were on the Huguenots' side at first, but once that line ended and Louis XIII took over, the Huguenots' political organization was broken up and their political assemblies forbidden. Then they were on their heels, and community was not enough.[8] Given this history, the Huguenots would strongly encourage Christians today to work for a godly Christian magistrate, especially when we see oppression on the horizon.

Another book that has been very influential in promoting Christian community is Dietrich Bonhoeffer's *Life Together.* I recommend his book. Bonhoeffer has a lot of good to say about the spiritual bond we have in Christ. It's an exhortation of faithful living. However, we should realize his book was not written to help us build comprehensive civilization. For example, Bonhoeffer says we should be content having spiritual community if we are geophysically scattered.[9] I agree that if God scatters us, we should be content. But I also see no reason why Christians should not proactively try to live together and to build Christendom. Bonhoeffer's community is good, it's just not enough to reach comprehensive Christianity.

Comprehensiveness Is a Requirement for Today

Comprehensive Christianity is true Christianity. We in the Reformed camp generally agree that Christ rules every area of life. We love quoting Kuyper. But have we considered this applies to us *now*? If we are truthful with ourselves, haven't we relegated comprehensiveness to the future, to being an "end" of the Christian Campaign?

I think we should take another look to realize that this is a *present-day* requirement. Comprehensiveness is not a goal for the future, as we tend to think. Although there will be progressive sanctification (Isa. 11:9; 1 Cor. 15:25), the blessings and cursings of Deuteronomy 27 and 28 are presented as current requirements to achieve current conditions. This is critical because whether you are under current blessings or curses determines a trajectory for the future.

I want to address a possible objection. Some people may think that the commands for the comprehensiveness of Israel apply merely to the church and not to all of society. With this view, all we have to do is correct the church, maybe even just a local congregation of a church, to meet these requirements. But there are two reasons this is not true.

First, the Hebraic Republic was given as an example for all nations (Deut. 4:5-8). It was not just the "true Israel" within Israel[10] that was commanded to obey and was placed on display. It was not a subset of Israel; it was the whole nation together. Just as all of Israel was required to comprehensively keep God's commands, so today our entire society—not just the Church—must do likewise.

Second, the scope of the commands of Deuteronomy 27 and 28 are not restricted to the church. They are actually more individual, family, and civil than ecclesiastical. In other words, the imperative given to Israel was specifically *societal*. And it was for all nations, then and now.

We can also look at this from a *blessings* angle. Since God demands comprehensiveness today, He also offers blessings for that comprehensiveness today. These contemporary blessing hold out an opportunity to put our families on a good course.

Comprehensiveness Does Not Mean Perfection

This is a crucial point. The comprehensiveness demanded in the Bible for earthly blessings is not one of perfection. Perfection is not going to happen this side of Glory. It is reserved to eternity future. But on the way to perfection, we should have *solidarity*. In other words, society needs to be comprehensively under the sway of one Lord and King —under one law (Ex. 12:49; Lev. 24:22; Num. 15:29). It means there is no other competing "system," as Kuyper put it.

The Christendom of old is a good example in that it was comprehensive and unified with a common religion. It was this medieval vision of a Christian society that the Puritans inherited, according to J. I. Packer. Speaking of the handoff from medievalism to the Puritans, he writes:

> Their vision of reality was not fragmented; they did not need to argue the point that Christian concern may not be limited to church order or to the welfare of individuals, but must embrace both together, along with the politics, economics, and culture of nations.[11]

The Christendom of old was far from perfect, especially in its theology. But it was comprehensive.

Going back to the example of Joshua in his conquest of Canaan, he "took the whole land," and "the land rested from war" (Josh. 11:23). But later, we see that much of the land remained to be possessed (13:1) and that Israel did not fully drive out the Canaanites (18:13). The book of Joshua has no problem saying that the mission was accomplished, that the land rested from war, and yet there was more to do.[12] The fact is that the Promised Land was comprehensively—but not perfectly—won by Israel.

Jon Acuff wrote a little book called *Finish: Give Yourself the Gift of Done*. He points out that what prevents people from reaching their goals is not a failure to start, lack of discipline, bad time management, or any of the other things we typically think. The biggest thing that prevents people from finishing, he says, is *perfectionism*. Perfectionism prevents starting because *you don't want to start until you're sure you can do it perfectly*. If you do manage to start, perfectionism causes people to stop midstream. If you miss one workout or eat one cheeseburger, you blew it. "Upon missing one day, I will quit the whole endeavor," writes Acuff.[13] And if you are fortunate enough to make it almost to completion, perfectionism will delay the finish because you're not sure it's going to be good enough.

Acuff's book highlights one of the hindrances that may prevent us from stepping forward in Kingdom work. When we recognize the comprehensiveness demanded by the Bible and then look around and see a society fragmented with multiple religions and law-breaking, we may be tempted to never even take a step. Or maybe we do take steps but defer comprehensiveness to the far future.

Let's remember: the old Christendom was not perfect.

And the new, local Christendom advocated for in this book will not be perfect. The Bible doesn't want us to be paralyzed by lack of perfection. Joshua's conquest of Canaan wasn't perfect, yet the land was considered by God and by the people to be conquered. Christ will do His work over time, but we should not delay comprehensive Christianity until the whole nation or world is converted.

We return to what Kuyper said at Princeton. Calvinism has not attained the level of a "life-system." Paganism, Romanism, and Islamism had attained this level in broad measure. As these systems played out their seasons, Calvinism was ready to take over, but modernism stole the stage (Kuyper thanks the French for that, mainly). And now modernism is set in our society like rebar-laden concrete.

Kuyper pointed out that Calvinism is the only "system" that is in line with God's design. John Calvin and those following in his vein searched the Scriptures and found that Christianity is a package deal. When all three social institutions are working together the way they are designed (*instituted* by God), we have a balanced three-bladed propeller. This "life-system" is indeed a City on a Hill, making others jealous.

In the rest of his lectures on Calvinism, Kuyper showed the beauty of a righteous, comprehensive society living under the Lordship of Jesus.

Cornelius Van Til wrote of comprehensive Christianity, "with Kuyper I believe that unless we press the crown rights of our King in every realm, we shall not long retain them in any realm."[14] Kuyper nailed comprehensiveness.

He knew, as Van Til did, Christianity is simply a package deal that must be fought for today.

What I think Kuyper missed was the idea that comprehensiveness happens in pockets along the way. He was searching for a worldwide "life-system" that had the organic, broad scope like paganism, for example. But the reason those other life-systems were so broadly accepted, almost all at once, is that they were according to the fallen nature of man and of the world. They were (and are) the default position, and it is easy to have a wide-spread comprehensive adherence to the default.

I appreciate that Kuyper wanted to fight the big systems of Romanism and modernism with a big system of Calvinism. But the Kingdom grows from small to big. In the military, we start from the "fighting unit" and go up. Fighting units are where tactics happen. A fighting unit is a group of about 50-200 men, small enough for one commander to get his arms around. For the Romans, it was the Centuria of about 80 men, which is what we see with the centurion of Matthew chapter eight. These fighting units are small, but they are comprehensive.

For American society, the fighting unit is the county. Rushdoony said the beauty of the American system is that it was built at the county level.[15] At the county level, we have an opportunity to be truly comprehensive. And if we can meet the current commands for comprehensiveness, we have a way for Kingdom realization. This will be a local life-system, on the way to Kuyper's view of a global life-system.

6

SOCIAL CONFESSIONALISM

There is no impropriety—no incompatibility with the
gospel dispensation—for a community to engage socially
in covenant.[1]

REV. DAVID SCOTT

Hundreds of Christians gathered in a field in
Ashland, Ohio in late summer of 2020 for an
important event. Local church and elected officials had
called an assembly, called the people to prayer and repentance. During the event, Ashland Mayor Matt Miller dedi-
cated the city to Jesus Christ, and County Commissioner
Emmitt Justice asked God for forgiveness of the sins the
county had committed against Him. People from all walks
of the local society were there. They called it a sacred
assembly. Mayor Miller said:

> As I stand before you tonight, in the bright light of His
> Son, to the extent I am able, I give this city of Ashland to

the Lord Jesus Christ. May this be a land where He rules supreme.[2]

State Representative Darrell Kick said, "I am not aware of another district where the mayor commits the city to Jesus Christ and a county commissioner asks forgiveness for the sins of the county."

What the people of Ashland, Ohio did was nothing new, even though it may seem like it. The concept of civil, church, and family representative heads confessing and covenanting as a geophysical and comprehensive society has a rich history, and it has direct Scriptural support.

Social Confessionalism

We now come to the nucleus of the confessional county. Social confessionalism is the "way" of removing curses and securing blessings for whoever is in that society. Wherever there is an institutional society, bound together comprehensively, confessing and covenanting with Jesus Christ, they have an opportunity to become a people and a place that is called by His name. Of course, individuals and the church are already called by His name. But here we are speaking about a society itself set apart for Jesus Christ.

I take the term "Social Confessionalism" from Reverend David Scott (1794-1871). He used the term "Social Covenanting," which means about the same since we covenant by confession. Born and educated in Scotland, Scott came to America in 1829 and brought his theology and his heritage of all-of-society covenanting with him. It is evident from his writings that Scott realized, even in the mid-1800s, America had lost this doctrine and practice.

Scott wrote vigorously to revive social covenanting because he saw it as essential to Christian life and civilization.

Here is the logic of confessionalism:

> Only by Christ's power can we begin to have a righteous society. Only by covenant is Christ's power available to us. The covenant required for this is a social covenant.

Another way of saying this is:

> Societal curses are caused by societal sins and are only removed by societal confession.

Similar to personal salvation and sanctification, a society needs God's grace. This is why we see, over and over, the concept of God being the God *of a people* and why we see people assembling and covenanting with God as a society (Ex. 19:7-8; Lev. 26:42; Deut. 4:6, 12:12-15; 29:1; 30:19; Josh. 1:16; 24:14-25). Covenanting with God is the only way to find mercy and truth. "All the paths of the LORD are mercy and truth unto such as keep his covenant and his testimonies" (Ps. 25:10).

Some agree about the need for God's grace and the need for a covenant but then say the covenant is administered through individuals, families, and churches. These elements, they say, comprise a totality of society. In other words, society is made up of the parts, and each of those parts has a covenant with God. Therefore a social covenant is not necessary. There are a number of problems with this view.

First, to determine how to have a righteous society, we

must look to the examples in Moses, Joshua, the good kings of Israel and Judah, and the post-exilic prophets. Here is our clearest blueprint of societies, specific examples of how to get right with God as a collective group. When we look at these examples, we see all-of-society confessionalism as a way to tap into God's power. The rulers called a sacred assembly, read the terms of the covenant, and they made their decision—they "stood to the covenant." There is a pattern here.

Second, Christ specifically instituted the civil magistrate as a representative head of a nation or society. We have to do this God's way. If He instituted three societal governments,[3] we cannot arbitrarily apply confessional requirements to only two of them.

Third, since the ascension and coronation of Christ, the expectations and requirements of civil magistrates to confess Christ have *increased*. Some think that national and all-of-society confessionalism was only for Israel and only for the old covenant. That is simply not true. A significant element of the gospel is proclaiming to civil leaders that they have a new Boss. Nations who fail to openly and officially recognize this new framework are held in derision (Ps. 2). In chapter four, "Christ's Mediatorial Reign," we saw this was a critical component of the early church's approach. It was probably the reason why Constantine confessed Christ the way he did. What we are saying is that we need to recover the Bible's perspective that God sees societies (i.e., nations, states, counties and towns) as distinct entities. He sees them in parts but also as a whole. And they have distinct covenant responsibilities as a whole.

Biblical Support for Social Confessionalism

A good portion of the biblical support for social confessionalism is based upon examples rather than direct commands. While we know that the moral law is still to be followed (Matt. 5:17; Rom. 7:7) and that the case law, as part of the moral law, is still in effect (Matt. 15:4), the normative element of *examples* is not as clear-cut. So what about the examples we see of Israel in the old covenant? Does God expect us to follow those examples? We can see the answer in the relationship between the Decalogue and the case law. The Decalogue provides the baseline ethical principles, and the case law is an illustration of those principles.[4] It is the *principle* that is binding, not the particular application. Therefore we are not constrained to follow the exact examples of Israel, but we must adhere to the principles they put into action, if they were approved examples.

In the Pentateuch, we see the ethical *principles* of social confessionalism. We see God's grace given to draw a people to Himself (Ex. 20:2), the idea of representative headship (Gen. 3:9; Ex. 34:1-2), the exercise of public confession (Lev. 16:21), and God's requirement for a nation to be righteous (Ex. 19:6).

When Israel puts God's commands into practice wisely, the nations will hear the statutes and understand how great a nation Israel is. Deuteronomy 4:5-8 shows us that God is pleased when other nations follow Israel's example of faithful living:

> Behold, I have taught you statutes and judgments, even as
> the LORD my God commanded me, that ye should do so
> in the land whither ye go to possess it. Keep therefore and
> do them; for this is your wisdom and your understanding

in the sight of the nations, which shall hear all these statutes, and say, Surely this great nation is a wise and understanding people. For what nation is there so great, who hath God so nigh unto them, as the LORD our God is in all things that we call upon him for? And what nation is there so great, that hath statutes and judgments so righteous as all this law, which I set before you this day?

Not only does this passage show that all nations should follow Israel's patterned examples; it shows that all nations *at all times* should do that. In other words, God is showing His desire for nations even outside of the old covenant and thus for all nations today. With this understanding, that Israel's faithful examples are models for all societies for all times, we can now evaluate those examples.

As God's redemptive plan unfolds and the Israelites come out of Egypt, we get a vivid example of social confessionalism in real history. We begin our study in Exodus 19 where Israel becomes a nation proper, a people called out to God. They had been God's people already under the patriarchs, but here the covenant is solidified. John Gill says, "They become a body politic, a free state, a commonwealth governed by its own laws, and those laws of God's making; yea, they should be a kingdom to him."[5] They did this by socially covenanting. God presented the condition, obedience and covenant-keeping (Ex. 19:6), and He presented the construct, an opportunity to sign up and become "a peculiar treasure unto me above all the people." The people took God up on His offer and confessed publicly:

And Moses came and called for the elders of the people, and laid before their faces all these words which the

LORD commanded him. And all the people answered together, and said, All that the LORD hath spoken we will do. And Moses returned the words of the people unto the LORD. (Exodus 19:7-8)[6]

This social covenant was unique in that it started the nation of Israel, but it wasn't a one-and-done event. It was the first of other social covenants. In fact, in Deuteronomy 29, we have the same people renewing the covenant they made earlier. This covenant renewal comes after a greater explanation of the law-covenant in Deuteronomy 28 where God gives a more extensive view of blessings and curses. Israel, presented with this information, covenanted *again:*

These are the words of the covenant, which the LORD commanded Moses to make with the children of Israel in the land of Moab, *beside the covenant which he made with them in Horeb.* (Deuteronomy 29:1, emphasis added)

That he may establish thee *today* for a people unto himself, and that he may be unto thee a God, as he hath said unto thee, and as he hath sworn unto thy fathers, to Abraham, to Isaac, and to Jacob. (Deuteronomy 29:13, emphasis added)

Notice that this established them as a people "today" unto God for a second time. That is important. It means societies can opt in or get a redo if they can meet the construct presented in social covenants. Remember, we are looking at approved examples, normative for all societies.

Another important point is that this renewed covenant reached back through Jacob and Isaac and landed at Abraham, and the Abrahamic covenant is the very same covenant that the new covenant church is plugged into today (Acts 2:39; Gal. 3:29). You can start to see how social confessions were not just for Old Testament Israel. The model is still available in the new covenant.

These social confessions continue to show up, often at momentous times. For example, before they entered the Promised Land, the people covenanted under Joshua (Josh. 1:16-18). And they did it again after conquering the Promised Land when Joshua challenged the people to "choose this day whom ye will serve." The people chose God publicly, and they made a public covenant (Josh. 24:24-25). Joshua said, "but as for me and my house, we will serve the LORD" (v. 15). We rightly use this verse to show fathers they have a covenantal responsibility for leading their families. But notice that the Israelites did not go back to their houses so that each family could make its own decision before God. Verses 16, 24, and 25 show us that they responded to Joshua's challenge *as a society of families*, not just as families.

Israel also practiced social confessionalism under the kingships of Jehoiada (2 Kin. 11:17), Josiah (2 Kin. 23:3), and Asa (2 Chr. 15:9, 12). Their stories show a similar pattern. The law was presented in some form, the kings and the people became convicted of their sin, and they obligated themselves to God and to change their ways.[7]

Interestingly, all these social covenants are presented as options to the people. The people could opt in to this deal, but they had to do it all together. In every case, it was a societal option, not an individual one. The covenant blessings and curses of Deuteronomy 28 came upon a collective, confessing and covenanting society. We have to reset our minds to this type of thinking if we hope to get off the track we are currently on. We need to return to the Bible's view that societies (nations, towns, etc.) are seen as collective covenantal units.

We Can Still Confess under Higher Civil Authority

You may be wondering: can we exercise social confessionalism as demonstrated by Israel in our God-hating environment? What about the political framework of the US today? Well, Ezra and Nehemiah provide the answer by showing us that, as a smaller society, they found God's blessing through social confessionalism. They did this even though they were under a heathen nation. This construct parallels that of a county in the US being under a heathen nation construct today.

Here's the story. Ezra returned to the land to build the temple, and Nehemiah later returned to build the wall. Both give us explicit examples of social confessionalism amid a people set against God. Whereas Moses, Joshua, and the kings had no higher governmental authority to contend with since they were their own nation, Ezra and Nehemiah's band had some significant hassle. At one point, they had to stop work for a decade (Ezra 4:24). Even though the Persian kings Cyrus and later Darius were benevolent kings whose hearts were turned by God, they were still running a heathen nation. Furthermore, in addition to the king, the land's local governors were heathen and very oppressive (Ezra 4:6-23; Neh. 4:1). Their *modus operandi* was similar to the statism of today. They turned to the centralized government to impose their will and demoralize God's people. They tattled to king Artaxerxes, writing:

> Be it known now unto the king, that, if this city be builded, and the walls set up again, then will they not pay toll, tribute, and custom, and so thou shalt endamage the revenue of the kings. (Ezra 4:13)

Yet in this environment, social confessionalism still happened. In the eighth chapter of Nehemiah, Ezra brings the law and preaches to "all the people" assembled together. They repent and commit to faithful observance of God's commands. Ultimately, they make a social covenant with all the representative heads of the civil magistrate (Neh. 10:1), the church (Neh. 10:2-13), and heads of households (Neh. 10:28). The story climaxes with this event:

> They clave to their brethren, their nobles, and entered into a curse, and into an oath, to walk in God's law, which was given by Moses the servant of God, and to observe and do all the commandments of the LORD our Lord, and his judgments and his statutes. (Nehemiah 10:29)

The overall approach of Ezra and Nehemiah is worth emulating. They trusted in God in the midst of their enemies. They did not unnecessarily provoke their enemies, and they spoke with respect to the heathen leaders, but nevertheless, they covenanted with God. Most importantly for our situation today, they confessed as a society under a heathen-nation construct, without permission. We have biblical warrant for doing the same thing as a county—without the permission of the state or federal government. We will discuss how this can be done later, but it does not have to be done officially, on government letterhead. Social covenanting runs straight to God (through Christ) and does not require permission from man.

Even the Lord's Prayer is confessional. Have you ever noticed that it does not say "My Father, who art in heaven" or "Give me this day my daily bread"? Rather, we see a corporate flavor. God is "*Our* Father." I am not saying you need a societal covenant to pray the Lord's Prayer. God's people are also individuals and families and churches. My point is that we may be missing the corporate aspect of our relationship to God.

Our particular topic, social confessionalism, is the textile of God's civilizations. Moses' covenant renewal and the other renewed covenants show us we have the opportunity to assemble and start afresh with God. It seems this can be done as often as necessary for societies to return to good standing with King Jesus. These social confessions are ultimately based in the Abrahamic covenant, which is fulfilled in Christ and available to us today.

And we don't have to wait until the nation is openly supportive. That is good news because the Bible presents pockets of righteous societies as a "way" of Kingdom realization more than an "end." We can, like Ezra and Nehemiah's societies, go ahead and covenant as soon as possible. *We don't even need permission.* In fact, since Jesus now owns all nations and He is our mediator, we are in a better position today eschatologically than Ezra and Nehemiah were.

However, we must remember that in every single case these confessions were all-of-society and performed with the covenantal heads of all three institutions assenting. Scotland's Covenanters followed this pattern. Their written confessions were precisely and thoroughly social. They got that idea from the Bible. In their "Solemn Acknowledgement of Publick Sins, and Breaches of the Covenant," (previously mentioned) they acknowledged and followed the pattern of social confession, "having the example of God's people of old."[8] We can look to the Covenanters as examples, but when we do, we should remember they were looking to the social confessionalism of the Bible as their example.

7

NATIONAL CONFESSIONALISM, MODIFIED FOR COUNTY

God wants our collective as well as our individual
obedience.[1]
William Edgar

A kind of evil could be felt everywhere and by
everyone in the 1850s and early 1860s. It was well-
accepted that the impending War Between the States
would be a punishment from God. People differed only in
their opinion about who was being punished and for what
reason.

Just before the war, in Xenia, Ohio—a location not far
from Ashland, Ohio, where they confessed Jesus Christ in
2020—men from the Reformed Presbyterian Church in
North America (RPCNA) had concluded something
surprising. They concluded that our primary national sin
was that we never confessed Christ as Lord. Our constitution, they concluded, failed to perform its greatest purpose:

to covenant our nation with God. They wrote the following:

> We regard the neglect of God and His law, by omitting all acknowledgment of them in our Constitution, as the crowning original sin of the nation, and slavery as one of its natural outgrowths. Therefore, the most important step remains yet to be taken—to amend the Constitution so as to acknowledge God and the authority of His law; . . We suggest the following as an outline of what seems to us to be needed in the preamble of that instrument, making it read as follows (proposed amendment in brackets):
>
> WE, THE PEOPLE OF THE UNITED STATES, [recognizing the being and attributes of Almighty God, the Divine Authority of the Holy Scriptures, the law of God as the paramount rule, and Jesus, the Messiah, the Savior and Lord of all,] in order to form a more perfect union . . . do ordain and establish this Constitution for the United States of America.[2]

Could they have been right? Is the lack of acknowledgment of God and His law the "crowning original sin of the nation"? In America's founding, did we fail to do the most important thing?

This movement to covenant with Christ in our constitution continued to grow during the war. Blood in the streets tends to bring out strenuous thinking and prayer. This new doctrine (it was "new" to the US in the 1850s but would not have been new in the 1650s) was heralded by what eventually became known as the National Reform Association, the NRA. That's right. The original NRA was about Reform, not Rifles. It had a much more ambitious agenda than allowing us to keep guns in our house, as important as that is. The NRA (the original one) has continued to this day in various forms. They produced a journal titled *The Christian Statesmen* from 1867 to 2008, a run which outlasted even *Life Magazine* (1883 to 2000). The movement could not be ignored during the war. It even gained an audience with President Lincoln. The members of the NRA were advocating the elimination of slavery and the above amendment to the constitution. Lincoln told the leaders of the NRA, "Gentlemen, in your former visit you requested of me two things. During the first term of my administration I was able to secure your first request. It is my hope that during my second term I will be able to secure your second request."[3] Lincoln lived forty-two days into his second administration. This was the last time it was on a US president's desk.

This chapter is about national confessionalism. National confessionalism points to the civil magistrate's obligation to confess Christ as Lord of their nation officially. As we will see, social confessionalism (all-of-society) and national confessionalism (civil magistrate) complement each other very well. Both are essential to the confessional county.

New Testament Confessionalism

After Jesus' resurrection, all authority was given to Him in heaven and on earth, and the natural expression of that authority was His disciples going forward with the comfort that Jesus would be with them to the end of the age. Their message was that of salvation but also of the kingship of Christ. Peter's sermon at Pentecost, the primordial Christian sermon, climaxed with the critical point that David is not king; Jesus is, and He will reign until He makes all His enemies His footstool (Acts 2:34-35). The closing phrase to the sermon caused the Israelites to be pricked in their heart. That closing line was this:

> Therefore let all the house of Israel know assuredly, that God hath made that same Jesus, whom ye have crucified, both Lord and Christ. (Acts 2:36)

"Both Lord and Christ" is important here. The gospel brings a new societal order as well as salvation.

The disciples were to preach Jesus as King to the people, and they were to preach Him as King *to existing kings*. Jesus said to His disciples, "ye shall be brought before governors and kings for my sake, for a testimony against them and the Gentiles" (Matt. 10:18). Jesus, speaking to Paul on the road to Damascus, said that Paul was "to bear my name before the Gentiles, and kings" (Acts 9:15).[4]

Acts 17 is an excellent example of the early church's message that Jesus is Lord and Christ. In Thessalonica, Paul brought an unwelcome announcement that would "turn the world upside down" (v. 6). What was this announcement that would bring a new world order? Paul was accused of "saying that there is another king, one Jesus" (v. 7).[5] After being forced to leave Thessalonica, and after a short stay in Berea, Paul arrives at Athens and finds it "wholly given to idolatry" (v. 16). (As we discussed earlier, idolatry is not allowed based on God's ownership of the world, which is now extended to Jesus. Jesus asked—and received—ownership of the heathen nations; Ps. 2:8). Athens was the epicenter of idolatry, and Paul takes it head on because of the crown rights of King Jesus. Paul gives the message that Jesus made the world and that He is "Lord of heaven and earth" (v. 24). In other words, the people of Athens must obey His earthy rule. Paul says, "And the times of this ignorance God winked at; but now commandeth all men every where to repent" (v. 30). God is demanding obedience to His law-word. Paul's sermon comes to a close with this message:

> Because he hath appointed a day, in the which he will judge the world in righteousness by that man whom he hath ordained; whereof he hath given assurance unto all men, in that he hath raised him from the dead. (Acts 17:31)

In this closing line, Paul presented the gospel's offer of salvation. We don't want to say that Paul was only talking about obedience to earth's new King. He was also talking about man's salvation. And actually, these two go together. Jesus' kingship was indispensable to this gospel message, especially for idolatrous cities. They could not have their idolatry and Jesus. Paul gives the reason: "Because he hath appointed a day, in the which he will judge the world in righteousness by that man whom he hath ordained."

Jesus will judge the world, which means He's in charge of the Gentile nations now. The society of Athens has to get rid of its idolatry and commit to Christ.

This doctrine is not lost on Paul's protege Timothy who, in one of the most beautiful benedictions in the Bible, heralds the kingship of Christ.

Now unto the King eternal, immortal, invisible, the only wise God, be honour and glory for ever and ever. Amen. (1 Timothy 1:17).

Biblical Arguments for National Confessionalism

The arguments for national confessionalism are simple yet strong. The mediatorial reign of Jesus Christ is one that specifically calls for nations to "Kiss the Son." Otherwise, they are held in derision (Ps. 2:4). The Father has set Jesus at His right hand, "far above all principality, and power, and might, and dominion, and every name that is named, not only in this world, but also in that which is to come: and hath put all things under his feet, and gave him to be the head over all things to the church, which is his body, the fulness of him that filleth all in all" (Eph. 1:21-23).

Proponents of national confessionalism have shown, quite convincingly, that the whole Bible has a theme of confessionalism. The mediatorial reign of Christ includes that of the civil magistrate (Ps. 2:6-12; 110:1-2; Dan. 7:13-14; Isa. 9:6-7; Acts 2:33-36; Matt. 28:18; Eph. 1:20-22; Phil. 2:9-11).[6] They emphasize the requirement for all nations to officially declare allegiance today to Jesus Christ in their public documents. The proponents also want to "devise political structures and policies that honor God and promote His justice."[7] National confessionalism is focused on the civil magistrate. It does not ignore the all-of-society ingredient, but it does not necessarily see it as an entry point. An entry point can be the civil magistrate confessing, and Hezekiah's example provides support that a civil ruler can secure societal blessing if he is faithful (2 Chr. 32:12, 21-23).

Local Christendom Today

Social confessionalism and national confessionalism can both be exercised in the confessional county. If we take the Christendom of old and refashion it locally by God's grace, we stand to find success as Joshua did by keeping all the commandments. The concept of Christendom brings both types of confessionalism together such that one could not imagine them separate. We have already made the case for social confessionalism. I think William Symington is right on point when he asks the following regarding a national confession:

> A nation, being a moral subject of Messiah, is as much bound to make profession of religion as any private individual whatever. Can that be a Christian nation which makes no profession of the religion of Christ? And how can such a profession be *nationally* made but in some way as we have supposed, namely, by the functionaries of the nation, in their official capacity, giving their authoritative sanction to the church's creed?[8]

A nation is bound to make profession of religion *just as much as an individual is.* I ask you, dear reader, to stop and think about this again. Could it be true that God requires nations to confess Him, and that the "functionaries" are the ones to confess? If this is true, can there be any doubt that where we are today could be (*has to be*) because of our disobedience to officially confess? I follow Symington's question with my own: If national confessionalism is a requirement, and if God also sees subordinate governments as distinct, can we not perform this duty at the county level? After all, we have "functionaries," and the

Bible shows that God historically deals with subordinate societies distinctly.

As discussed earlier, Constantine and Napoleon are often regarded as the bookends of Christendom. During this time, kings *confessed Christ.* Constantine was first. He publicly confessed Jesus as the Messiah, the King of kings, thus beginning Christendom. Charlemagne did the same on Christmas Day, AD 800, when Pope Leo III crowned him as Roman emperor. This tradition continued until 1804, when Napoleon reversed course and crowned himself king.[9]

The bound-together society of Christendom was not an invention. It was simply the Christian Gentile nations following the example of God's people outlined in the Old Testament. The new Christian nations looked to the Hebraic Republic for their model. There was a covenantal connection of society. Isaiah shows how rulers and subjects are bound together, and he calls them to a common obedience:

> Hear the word of the LORD, ye *rulers* of Sodom; give ear unto the law of our God, ye *people* of Gomorrah. (Isaiah 1:10, emphasis added)

Notice how Isaiah flows so fluidly from the rulers to the people. Furthermore, the rulers and the people share a common reward if they are obedient. The reward is this:

> If ye be willing and obedient, ye shall eat the good of the land. (Isaiah 1:19)

Isaiah shows us here that all the people in a society are to commit themselves to God, but the rulers get special mention as the representative heads. It is a good example of combining social and national confessionalism (it is also a good example of *local* confessionalism). For the rest of this book, when I write, "social confessionalism," I am bringing in the national confessionalism element as well. Since Jesus is now reigning over "nations"[10] in the new covenant, any social confessionalism would require the civil magistrate to confess Him as King.

Despite the faithful efforts of the National Reform Association, our constitution still remains the same. We have no outward, official acknowledgment of Jesus' kingship over our country. What prevented the early NRA from getting what they desired? Most likely, the nation was too far down the track of pluralism for it to gain popular support, even in the 1860s. Or perhaps God had run out of patience and decided (as He sometimes does) to go ahead and punish us by walking contrary to us (Lev. 26:24).

But the principles of national confessionalism remain today and are becoming more and more relevant. One hundred and seventy years of steady scholarship generated a rich history, and the vast writings on the subject are ready for the taking. In the past three decades, there has been a rejuvenation of the doctrine by such authors and preachers as William Einwechter, P. Andrew Sandlin, and William Edgar. They speak to the issues today in a powerful and faithful way. Like in the years before the War Between the States, our nation is divided and under what seems to be a growing judgment. So we should not give up the fight for national confessionalism.

In both national and social confessionalism, *the confes-*

sion comes early. These doctrines stand or fall on the confession requirement as a "way," not an "end" of Kingdom realization. Only with a covenant in place can we even *begin* to please God and tap into His power. Since we did not confess Christ openly in our national constitution, national confessionalism seeks to remedy that wrong. However, I believe the confessional county can utilize the doctrine sooner, and perhaps it can put us on a shorter path to national confession.

8

OTHER SOCIETAL APPROACHES

In chapter three, we saw that the US is under land curses. A land curse is God's punishment against society for societal sins. God sees societies as a whole and holds them accountable for actions within their jurisdiction and borders. We also saw that being under a curse means that a society will not go forward in societal, earthly blessings unless (1) God determines the curse has punished us enough or (2) we confess as a comprehensive society under representative headship. With the dire situation that we cannot get into "blessing territory" until we get out of "curses territory," we should be searching the Bible diligently to find a way to do this. We should be looking up to God, pointing to multiple Bible passages, and humbly asking Him, "Will this work? Will this please You? Will this help my grandchildren?"

In other words, we are searching for biblical solutions because (as the *Benedict Option* shows) we lost the culture war. That doesn't mean God is not moving history forward to ultimate redemption. God didn't lose; He never does. God ordains all things according to His divine will.[1] And since God doesn't lose, neither do we ultimately (1 Cor. 15:57). But the Bible also warns us to be very concerned about our current society's standing before Him.

This chapter will discuss four other approaches: evangelism, claiming the promises of the Psalms, the doctrine of the remnant, and intercessory prayer by the church on behalf of the nation. These are gracious blessings and duties God gives to His people. There is no question that all of them are part of God's joint strategy to reconcile all things to Himself.

However, in my conversations with people about confessionalism, often I hear these approaches presented *in place of confessionalism*. People will assert that confessionalism is a beneficial result of evangelism, for example. We will see, as important and beneficial as these other approaches are, they do not make confessionalism unnecessary. Nor do they allow us to put confessionalism off to the future.

Evangelism

Like the other strategies we have been mentioning, evangelism is a "way" to achieve the "end" in Christ's campaign to put all enemies under His feet. It is, in fact, a gracious and strong weapon. When the Bible says God's Word is the sword of the Spirit, we need to remember that up until the late 1700s when the rifle began to be used in mass warfare, the sword was the most lethal weapon of any battle. Today, we might say the Word of God is the thermonuclear weapon of the Spirit. And, as the Westminster

Confession says, saving faith "is ordinarily wrought by the ministry of the Word."[2]

Saving a soul from eternal damnation—and, in doing so, making a new creation—is our main line of effort not only for the individual's sake but also for society. We are saved not only from hell but also from our sins. Only a new creature in Christ is able to keep the law in a way that pleases God; therefore the only way to have a truly righteous society is for hearts to be changed. I am not saying evangelism's goal is to have a righteous society. Evangelism's primary goal is the worship and glorification of God. I am saying that only a new creature in Christ can have an effective confession of any type—including social confession.

Evangelism enables social confessionalism; however, it does not replace it as a way to remove societal curses. When someone confesses Christ personally and is saved, Christ's atoning work is applied to them personally. Yet societal sins still require a separate, societal confession for a society to be forgiven. The land still has to be healed. That does not mean that a person is individually condemned for societal sins. A new creature in Christ is justified at conversion (Rom. 5:1) and will continue in sanctification and glorification (Rom. 8:28-30)—regardless of societal sins—and be saved in eternity. But God sometimes gives temporal, societal punishment in terms of land curses. In Deuteronomy 28:9, which is the pivot point between blessings and curses in that chapter, we read: "The LORD shall establish thee an holy people unto himself, as he hath sworn unto thee, if thou shalt keep the commandments of the LORD thy God, and walk in his ways." Calvin, commenting on this verse, says, "This refers indeed to earthly blessings."[3] If these are earthly blessings, surely their opposites are earthly curses. They are earth-bound and temporal in nature.[4]

We see the same concept with generational sins of the family. God only holds individuals accountable for their own sins. "The son shall not bear the iniquity of the father, neither shall the father bear the iniquity of the son" (Ezek. 18:20).[5] However, God will still visit "the iniquity of the fathers upon the children, and the children's children, to the third and to the fourth generation" (Ex. 34:7). A person may have family curses that are working against him. If so, he can confess those family sins, and God will remove them by applying the blood of Christ. Land curses, like family curses, are only temporal. But they still require confession, and they still require blood, which Jesus provides.

Going back to the idea that personal evangelism will not remove societal sins, we can prove this in two ways. First, when you confess Christ as your personal savior, you confess your own sins. There is no requirement to confess the sins of your father in order to be saved (John 3:16; Rom. 10:9; 1 John 1:9).[6] But in social confession, you are required to *confess generational sins* as well as individual. This secures earthly (temporal) forgiveness as a society. We see this in Leviticus:

> If they shall confess their iniquity, *and the iniquity of their fathers,* with their trespass which they trespassed against me, and that also they have walked contrary unto me;
> And that I also have walked contrary unto them, and have brought them into the land of their enemies; if then their uncircumcised hearts be humbled, and they then accept of the punishment of their iniquity: then will I remember my covenant with Jacob, and also my covenant with Isaac,

and also my covenant with Abraham will I remember; *and
I will remember the land.* (Leviticus 26:40-42, emphasis
added)

Here we see the assembly was to confess their iniquity
and the iniquity of their fathers. This is how the land will be
remembered in covenantal terms. It is important to note
that Leviticus 26 is in the context of social confessionalism. The "remember the land" of verse 42 hearkens back to
many verses of the land and the covenantal, relational
aspect of it. The whole chapter is about land curses and
blessings. Confession of *"the iniquity of their fathers"* is
required because societal sin has defiled the land, even if
from a previous generation. Personal salvation is different
in that it only requires confession for personal sins. We see
two different confessions (personal and social), with two
different effects (personal and societal), in two different
timelines (temporal and eternal).[7]

The second proof that personal evangelism will not
remove societal sins comes from our oft-cited prayer in 2
Chronicles. "If my people, which are called by my name,
shall humble themselves, and pray, and seek my face, and
turn from their wicked ways; then will I hear from heaven,
and will forgive their sin, and will heal their land" (2 Chr.
7:14). The first condition, "If my people, who are called by
my name," means they are God's people already.[8] That is
the *precondition*—twice emphasized—for God to hear their
prayer. There is no forgiveness and healing of the land
unless God is willing to listen, and He will only listen to
those people who are His.

We often miss the fact that this prayer is performed in a
social confession context. Chapters six and seven of
Second Chronicles are dealing with the same event, the

consecration of the temple, and we see a social covenanting pattern: "And the king turned his face, and blessed the whole congregation of Israel: and all the congregation of Israel stood" (2 Chr. 6:3). The fact that they were God's people was a precondition to approach God for societal forgiveness, but social confession was still required to secure forgiveness and heal the land.

Let's take a real town as an example: Mystic, Connecticut (pop. 4,249). Let's imagine the churches in Mystic started a Spirit-led evangelism ministry (and prayer ministry), and God blessed it such that He converted the whole town. According to the Bible, this would not remove any land curses the town was under. On the good side, it would enable the town to stop sinning and not pile any more curses on. It would also *lead them* to social confessionalism, which does forgive societal sins (in the past) and heals the land (for future blessings). So the town of Mystic is now full of reborn citizens (praise God). Now they are in a position to pray 2 Chronicles 7:14 and receive its promise in full measure. But land is not healed until they do.

We need to evangelize aggressively, and when we do, we need to remember that part of that gospel message is to keep all the commandments of Christ. We need to remember there is a national element to the gospel as well. As we saw in chapter seven of this book, the kingship of Christ was integral to the gospel presentations of the early centuries. Christ's Kingdom is not just spiritual; it is physical, tangible, earthy (Col. 1:20). When the Bible says that "nations" will be saved, it is very likely that a national confession would flow quickly and naturally behind personal salvation (Gen. 26:4; Job 12:23; Ps. 22:27; 102:15; Isa. 2:3-4; 11:12; Mic. 4:2; Luke 24:47). Put another way, a national confession would not save personally, but it would secure an earthly salvation in a national sense from curses. The nation would be blessed.

In sum, evangelism is our number one societal approach, but our evangelism needs to come in the way it did in the early church, with the powerful message that Jesus is both Lord and Christ (Acts 2:36). And we must remember that personal confession does not remove the societal sins of the land.

Promises in the Psalms

Some might agree that we are under land curses but quickly point to the Psalms as our way out. The Psalms, they would say, provide a way for God's people to be protected in the midst of enemies. The question for us here, however, is this: If we are under national land curses, can we claim promises of protection that are in the Psalms? I ask this because the protection in the Psalms is primarily written against enemies, not against curses. The Psalms declare protection of God's people from their enemies. They are not primarily written to protect God's people from judgment. For example, one of the societal curses we see in Leviticus 26:24 is that God will walk contrary to us. If God is walking contrary to us as a nation, can we sing the Psalms and find protection for ourselves as Christians?

The answer is yes. We can claim protection from the Psalms and other Scriptures even if under a national land curse. I see three reasons why. First, we mentioned Jeremiah 17 earlier. Here the nation of Judah is in sin and under punishment (vv. 1-4), yet God still promises to bless the man that trusts in the Lord (vv. 7-8). Second, in 2

Corinthians 1:20, we read that all the promises of God are yes and Amen for the Christian. Along with this, Christ is the mediator of a better covenant based on better promises (Heb. 8:6). God sealed us by the Holy Spirit and sent Him into the world, and Christ said He would never leave us (Matt. 28:20). Third, we are in one sense a distinct nation of Christians even though we are Americans. "But ye are a chosen generation, a royal priesthood, an holy nation, a peculiar people; that ye should shew forth the praises of him who hath called you out of darkness into his marvellous light" (1 Pet. 2:9). We have dual citizenship, with our primary citizenship being in heaven (Phil. 3:20).

So I believe, comparing Scripture with Scripture, we can claim the promises of protection from the Psalms even if our land is under a curse.

However, I would caution us in two areas. I would caution us against praying the psalms of national protection for the United States. We do not have a national covenant with Christ,[9] and even if we did, we have not been faithful to keep covenant with Him. We are at a point where we are celebrating blatant sin. In fact, if we invoke psalms of national protection for the US, we may be in danger of bringing God's wrath upon us because those psalms of protection are for Israel as a covenanted, faithful nation against the uncovenanted, unfaithful heathen nations (Ps. 46:6; 106:47).[10] Is there any doubt we are on the wrong side of that conflict? It would be presumptuous for us to claim psalms of national protection in our current condition.

I would also caution us not to use the Psalms' promises of protection as our long-term, primary strategy. At some point (and we may be very close to that point today), God's mercy for wayward societies wears out, and the only earthly protection God gives His people is warning and allowing them to flee (Gen. 19:15; Matt. 24:16; Luke 21:21). As good as protection is, we really want long-term blessings in the land if God will grant it.

The Psalms' protection is real, and we have real enemies, including Satan and his minions. The Psalms put God's power to work on our behalf. My main point is that they are not primarily focused on protection against God's curses. We can (and should) still ask for the protection of Psalm 37 and Psalm 91 and others, but overall, when dealing with the question of removing curses and securing blessings, we have to turn to the verses that deal with that directly.

The Doctrine of the Remnant

While the Psalms are not primarily interested in defending us against God's punishments for the wicked surrounding us, the doctrine of the remnant is specifically interested in that. The remnant is God's tool for preserving His people. And there are two ways He uses the remnant to preserve. First, He preserves a society from destruction. Second, He preserves a line of faithful people in order to continue His redemptive plan.

We see the preserving element of society with Sodom and Gomorrah and with Israel's 7,000 men who had not bowed a knee to Baal. Sodom and Gomorrah did not have a large enough remnant to satisfy God. Later in Israel, even though Elijah thought he was the only faithful one left, God had reserved 7,000 men. God would not allow the nation to be carried off in Elijah's time (although He would carry them off eventually). Isaiah also brings in the preserving element of the remnant: "Except the LORD of hosts had left unto us a very small remnant, we should have been as Sodom, and we should have been like unto Gomorrah" (Isa. 1:9). God has shown He is willing to preserve societies on behalf of the embedded remnant.

God also uses the remnant to preserve a line of faithful people so that His redemptive plan continues. In Romans 11:4, Paul pulls forward the remnant doctrine from Elijah's talk with God mentioned above. When asked if God was going back on His promise to preserve God's people in Israel, Paul responds, "Even so then at this present time also there is a remnant according to the election of grace" (Rom. 11:5). God maintains His plan by maintaining a godly line of people. As Gary North writes, "This remnant is sometimes a remnant of righteous covenant-keepers within a society of covenant-breakers."[11] In sum, the remnant can be saved even in the midst of broad punishment, thus allowing God's redemptive plan to continue.

But *how* does God protect the remnant? The plagues of Egypt provide an interesting study. God indeed protected Israel *among* the Egyptians. The Lord selectively killed only the Egyptian cattle (Ex. 9:3-4), and darkness was only over the Egyptians (10:23). However, for the plagues that were widespread in nature, such as weather or insect infestation, the Lord employed protection geographically. The Israelites were protected in the land of Goshen (8:22; 9:26). During the Passover, the Lord instituted a way for Israel not to be punished in the midst of the Egyptians. Since Christ is our Passover, it may be possible for Christians to claim this type of protection in the midst of a curse today.[12] However, once again, we need to remember that the initial Passover was so that God could *remove* His people out of Egypt. Likewise, Jesus told His believers in

Judea to flee to the mountains when He comes in judgment (Matt. 24:14-20). God can protect His remnant in many ways, but historically He has often done so by geographic separation.[13] I think the most likely reason is that the land was defiled. Without a doubt, God has a special place in His heart for the righteous minority. "The LORD did not set his love upon you, nor choose you, because ye were more in number than any people; for ye were the fewest of all people" (Deut. 7:7). Leviticus 26:44 is particularly relevant to us. Here God says that even in the land of enemies, He will not destroy His people utterly.[14] So the doctrine of the remnant is a great expression both of God's mercy, because it delays judgment, and of His faithfulness, because it saves a line of people and enables everlasting covenants.

The question for us is whether the doctrine of the remnant is a good *strategy* in post-Christian America. Is this something we can request from God and confidently claim to deliver us from curses? Is this something that we can keep in the back of our minds as we live and work and preach in a nation that celebrates blasphemy, sodomy, idolatry, Sabbath-breaking, and murder?

Like the promise of protection from the Psalms, the doctrine of the remnant is something we can pray for and trust God to answer. However, I don't think we should turn to it as our primary strategy. There are two reasons for this.

First, we do not know where the line is for a remnant to protect a larger society. We still do not know how many people would have saved Sodom; we only know it was at least ten people. We are not given the logic behind the 7,000 who preserved Israel (1 Kin. 19:18).[15] In Ezekiel 22:30, it seems only one man was required to deflect God's wrath. We do not know where the goalpost is. In America today, what is the percentage of faithful that would turn away or at least delay God's wrath? We simply don't know. We do not even know how many Americans today have not bowed the knee to modern Baals.

Second, the doctrine of the remnant is more a condition than a strategy. It preserves Christians for a later, larger advance (Jer. 31:7).[16] When God's people are in remnant status in the Bible, they can make progress and find success. Joseph and Daniel are good examples. And those in Babylon are told to build houses, plant gardens, and take wives. The reason given is: "that ye may be increased there, and not diminished" (Jer. 29:6). But in these situations, those in the remnant are simply exercising their faith in taking dominion (Joseph and also the Babylonian exiles, for example) and in pure worship (Daniel, for example). In other words, they are executing commands as a remnant; they are not exercising their remnant status.

I mention this because I am starting to hear people speak of the remnant as an optional strategy to take. They are (in my opinion) leaning toward "hunker" mode. Certainly we should be wise and prepare, and we should be ready to flee.[17] But we also have the promise that the gates of hell cannot hold up against the advancing church (Matt. 16:18). The remnant, then, is a condition, not a strategy. If God puts us in this condition, we should still focus on executing God's commands to cast down strongholds, and we should still seek ways for our land to be blessed.

Intercessory Prayer by the Church for the Nation

Sometimes as the church we pray intercessory prayers to confess the sins of the land. But I am not sure we have considered how the Bible presents intercessory prayers. Ezra's example is one case that shows the church is limited in its ability to confess the sins of the land; Ezra shows a confession by the entire society is needed. We will see that the church alone cannot secure forgiveness for society.

When Ezra's journey from Babylon ends and he is finally in Israel, he becomes aware that some of the people have disobeyed God by marrying the daughters of the land. Ezra was astonished. He fell on his knees and confessed the iniquity of the people (Ezra 9:5-15). He spread out his hands and poured out his heart "and said, O my God, I am ashamed and blush to lift up my face to thee, my God: for our iniquities are increased over our head, and our trespass is grown up unto the heavens" (Ezra 9:6). His prayer seems to cover all the bases.

Now, you would think that would be sufficient to secure forgiveness. Ezra is a priest after all, and boy, he sure prayed a good prayer! But the story goes on to show that after Ezra's confession, an assembly met (Ezra 10:1), and only after the *assembly's* confession and commitment to obedience are they on good covenantal standing with God (Ezra 10:9-12).

This brings up the question: why was the social confession necessary after Ezra's prayer? Wasn't Ezra's prayer enough? For our purposes here, can the church interpose for societal sins? When we pray 2 Chronicles 7:14, for example, can we find forgiveness such that God can "heal our land"? Upon detailed analysis, the intercessory examples of Abraham, Moses, Samuel, Daniel, and Jeremiah only secured *a temporary covering.*

Let's walk through these examples. Abraham pleaded for Sodom and Gomorrah and got a suspension of judgment (Gen. 18:23-33), but judgment still came because of the people's sin (Gen. 19:24). Abraham's prayer may have worked if there were more righteous in the city, but then we are into the doctrine of the remnant again, and we simply do not know how many is enough.

Moses had partial success. He interceded after the golden calf scandal (Ex. 32:10-14), but he only received a temporary suspension of judgment (v. 14). He interceded a second time for the same event after finding out how bad the idolatry was. Moses asked God to (1) forgive the people's sins or (2) to hold him personally accountable. God said no to both of Moses' requests (vv. 33-34), but He allowed the people to continue to the Promised Land.[18] He did not destroy them utterly or blot out the nation, but God still said He would judge them (v. 34), and He sent a plague among them, which is a land curse (v. 35). Moses did convince God to go with them into the Promised Land (Ex. 34:9-10). In the end, Moses' intercession granted temporal suspension of God's judgment.[19] It was significant, however, in that it allowed the nation to survive and enter the Promised Land.[20]

Aaron, under the direction of Moses, was able to stop a plague by interceding with a censer and fire from the altar (Num. 16:46-49), but the Lord had already killed 14,700 people.

Ezra, as we saw above, suspends judgment with his prayer, but it was the all-of-society confession that secured forgiveness.

Job intercedes for his family (Job 1:5), but we are not

told if this was efficacious to eternal forgiveness.[21] We only know that God approved of this. At the end of the book of Job, God says He will accept Job's intercessory prayer and forgive the folly of his accusers, but his accusers still have to bring their own sacrifices (Job 42:8). Applying this to the US, even if the church could pray for forgiveness of the nation, that prayer would need to be accompanied by national repentance.

Samuel tells the people to repent, which they did, but he leaves the responsibility with the people. "But if ye shall still do wickedly, ye shall be consumed, both ye and your king" (1 Sam. 12:25).[22] Samuel is important because he shows two things. First, *the church should intercede for the greater society.* Second, *this prayer cannot substitute for all-of-society confession.* Samuel basically prayed that the *people* would repent, and they did.[23]

Solomon's intercessory prayer seems to have been approved and answered by God in full measure (2 Chr. 7:1); however, his prayer was more representative than intercessory. This prayer was given before an assembly where everyone stood, "And the king turned his face, and blessed the whole congregation of Israel: and all the congregation of Israel stood" (2 Chr. 6:3). Solomon was praying with the people, not in place of them.

Daniel gives the most extensive intercessory prayer in the Bible. It is deeply moving. "We have sinned, and have committed iniquity, and done wickedly" (Dan. 9:5). He calls out with everything he has and asks for God to turn His anger away from His holy mountain (v. 16). Daniel prayed for Jerusalem to be saved (and by that he meant broader Israel). God answers Daniel by sending Gabriel. Gabriel says it is going to take seventy weeks of years, seventy times seven. There will be 490 years of preservation (temporary overlooking of sin). Then Jerusalem will still be destroyed (v. 26).[24] Ultimately, forgiveness is coming to God's elect (Rom. 11:5), but the transgression has to be finished and the Messiah has to come (Dan. 9:25).

We know that when the Messiah came, rather than a societal confession of Christ, Jerusalem had a societal crucifixion of Him (Acts 2:23, 36), and the blessing was extended to the Gentiles. Gabriel says the Messiah will bring in everlasting righteousness (Dan. 9:24), but not without great destruction first. Like the others, we see that Daniel's intercessory prayer did not fully turn God's wrath away, but it did provide a temporary covering. Only after the old covenant is done away with and a new Mediator put in place can civilization fully tap into those blessings.

In Jeremiah 7:16, we see that at some point intercessory prayer hits a wall: "Therefore pray not thou for this people, neither lift up cry nor prayer for them, neither make intercession to me: for I will not hear thee."

Elijah tried intercessory prayer the other way, against Israel rather than for them. God did not answer his prayer (Rom. 11:2-4).

Really the only One who prays intercessory prayers and gets everything He asks for is Jesus. That is not surprising since He's the only one worthy to open the book or to even look at it (Rev. 5:4).

I am not saying intercessory prayer does no good at all. It does much good. First Timothy 2:1-2 says we should pray intercessory prayer for "all men, for kings, and for all that are in authority; that we may lead a quiet and peaceable life in all godliness and honesty." Intercessory prayer seems to convince God to delay punishment, as with Moses and Daniel. It may buy some time for our nation to repent. Moses convinced God to allow some of God's people to enter the Promised Land. Daniel's intercessory prayer seems to have been answered eschatologically, and God preserved the people of God to bring in the Messiah.[25] Intercessory prayer can also lead a society to repentance, as demonstrated with Ezra and Samuel. But the society must still repent if they are under judgment. In other words, intercessory prayer can lead to social confession, but it cannot replace it.

When we as a church pray 2 Chronicles 7:14, we need to realize we (as the church) cannot secure the promise for the United States. Here is the verse:

> If my people, which are called by my name, shall humble themselves, and pray, and seek my face, and turn from their wicked ways; then will I hear from heaven, and will forgive their sin, and will heal their land. (2 Chronicles 7:14)

The "my people, who are called by my name" coincides with "their wicked ways" and "their land." It is not two separate sets of people, one interceding for another. The people who have committed the sins (which is a collective society) have to confess for the land to be healed.

God may grant temporary suspension of judgment by answering the church's prayer of 2 Chronicles 7:14, and He may soften the hearts to allow repentance. So I'm not saying the church should stop praying it. But we still need societal confession for societal sins. Ultimately, the only intercessory prayer we can trust *for forgiveness* is by the one mediator between God and man, the man Jesus Christ.[26] That is why we need to connect to Him as a society.

Evangelism is our primary weapon in Christ's campaign. But we cannot stop at evangelism. The Bible shows we still need societal confession for societal sins. Our evangelism has to include teaching the nations to obey all that Christ commanded, and that will (God willing) lead to societal confession. The Psalms lay out wonderful promises of blessings and protection for God's people, but they are not really designed for removing land curses and securing societal blessings. The doctrine of the remnant shows God's mercy and faithfulness; however, it is more a condition than a strategy. If God puts us in the remnant, we must pursue the duties of God that cast down strongholds. Finally, the church should intercede in prayer on behalf of the nation. Intercessory prayer can prolong God's mercy and lead to social confession. However, a church interceding on behalf of the nation will not secure societal forgiveness for societal sins.

Jeremiah used intercessory prayer and invoked the remnant doctrine at the same time: "O LORD, save thy people, the remnant of Israel" (Jer. 31:7). We should follow his example and preach these protections as great things the Lord has done and will do again. Yet social confessionalism, where representative heads of all of Christ's institutions repent and confess Christ, is the clearest, most focused model we have in the Bible for securing societal blessings, especially for those societies in current disobedience to God.

9

CONFESSIONAL COUNTY
STRATEGY

Without a strategy, facing up to any problem or striving
for any objective would be considered negligent.
SIR LAWRENCE FREEDMAN

W hen John Piper suggested a modification to the
Westminster Catechism's first question, what he
did was change our strategy on how to glorify God. This
first question of the Catechism asks, "What is the chief end
of man?" and it answers, "Man's chief end is to glorify God
and to enjoy him forever."

But Piper had an idea. He suggested we pull the *enjoy*
part *forward*. His version is this:

Man's chief end is to glorify God *by* enjoying him forever.
(emphasis added)

Notice what Piper did. He made the enjoyment of God
a way to glorify Him. In the strategy paradigm of "ways,
means, and ends," Piper changed enjoyment from an "end"

to a "way." The enjoyment is now an action item that accomplishes the whole purpose—to glorify God. It became a causal element, not a resultant one. (Piper is not saying that *any enjoyment* will please God or that God's grace is not needed. We need God's grace in Piper's model just as much as the Westminster model—perhaps more— because when you move our actions to a current timeline, you are moving them into sin-space. This side of eternity has sin in it, so we need lots of grace here.)

We preach Piper's construct often because it is so employable. By removing enjoyment as an end, God's glorification sticks out more. It is no longer our glorification and our enjoyment of God; it is just His glorification, giving us a singular target to shoot at. We also have something to shoot *with*. Now we have the arrow of enjoyment, something we can pick up and set on the string. In other words, we have something to do, and doing is important (Jas. 1:22).

The forthcoming confessional county strategy is where we pull things forward, placing them in our current day in a Piperian sort of way.

Christian Strategy

You're a strategist. You've been one since the age of three— maybe earlier. And you're probably a good one. Christians should be the best at strategy because strategy is the estimate and practice of *causation*. And we know what causation is: *causation is the law of harvest presented in the Bible*, reaping what you sow (Gal. 6:7). Because we have special revelation, Christians are the only ones who can account for the ultimate causation, which is God Himself. The humanists, with their empiricism, also know causality, but not as deeply as we do. For example, they know that bingeing on junk food causes bad health, but they do not know the reason behind it, that we are made in the image of God and we are to be stewards of our bodies. A junk food binge is bad because gluttony is bad and is out of line with God's creation. We reap bad health because God upholds a consistent causality which we see in Genesis 8:22, "While the earth remaineth, seedtime and harvest, and cold and heat, and summer and winter, and day and night shall not cease."

In upholding and utilizing biblical causation, we are not saying this is a mechanical, magic formula. The ways of God are higher than ours, many of them past finding out (Rom 11:33). There are the secret things. But those things that are revealed can be—*and should be*—taken advantage of:

> The secret things belong unto the LORD our God: but those things which are revealed belong unto us and to our children for ever, that we may do all the words of this law. (Deuteronomy 29:29)

We can also see the causal elements of strategy in nature. One reason the secularists are so good at strategy is that the stakes are high in real life, especially in real war. You become very interested in causality when your life is on the line.

Antoine Henri Jomini is one of those good strategists. As the protege of Napoleon, causation was at the heart of his writing. He was the one who codified the concept of the "decisive point," the point about which the battle would pivot. There is some science (and perhaps more art) in finding the decisive point. Jomini did not just want to determine the decisive point—he also wanted to get there. He tells us that getting to the decisive point can be, well, decisive. Jomini is the one who elevated logistics to the level of importance it enjoys in today's military doctrine. In my opinion, the thing that sets the US apart and gives us the best military in the world is not our ability to strike but our ability to move. Jomini would be pleased.

There's one more thing about strategy—timing. Timing relates to sequencing, which relates to causation. If we attack first, we estimate "RESULT A" should happen. If the enemy attacks first, we estimate "RESULT B" should happen. There are many sub-causations that flows out from here. Military strategists call these "branches and sequels." The point is that Piper, Clausewitz, Jomini, and all the rest of us strategists make a strategic decision when we determine where things go on a timeline.

Grand Strategy in The Great Commission

The Great Commission is our grand strategy. It has ways, means, and ends. It has causation and timing. It also has comprehensiveness and societal confessionalism, the two things we discussed in previous chapters. It should not surprise us that God packed all of the components into the Christian's famous charge:

> All power is given unto me in heaven and in earth. Go ye therefore, and teach all nations, baptizing them in the name of the Father, and of the Son, and of the Holy Ghost: Teaching them to observe all things whatsoever I

have commanded you; and lo, I am with you alway, even unto the end of the world. Amen. (Matthew 28:19-20)

In this Commission, we see comprehensiveness as a "way" and confessionalism as a "way." The teaching of "whatsoever I have commanded you" means totality is built into God's ethics. Here the Great Commission is similar to Joshua's commission. The book of the law was not to depart from Joshua's mouth that he may do "according to *all* that is written therein" (Josh. 1:8, emphasis added). With this comprehensiveness, Joshua will have success, and so will we.

Confessionalism is also a "way" in the Commission, and we see it in the baptism element. Jesus wants nations baptized. Of course, this does not diminish individual baptism. As we said earlier, evangelism is our sharpest weapon, and saving souls enables a society to be holistically set apart for God. In baptism, we confess and covenant to one God in three Persons. The Great Commission has individual salvation in mind, but it also extends beyond the individual. Teaching and baptizing nations has a societal element to it.

Confessionalism is present *intrinsically* in the Great Commission as the glue between the Commander and His army. Under Joshua, people rose to their commission and made a covenant to follow Joshua's commandments. They stood and committed themselves in this way: "According as we hearkened unto Moses in all things, so will we hearken unto thee: only the LORD thy God be with thee, as he was with Moses" (Josh. 1:17).

If comprehensiveness and confessionalism are the ways, what are the "means" in the Commission? In strategic phraseology, "means" are the resources that provide the ability to proceed. The means in the Commission are *Christ's power and His grace*. This is crucial to get. It is the *sine qua non* of confessionalism. It is Christ's power, not our own. The way to tap into that power is by way of covenant. When you combine this idea with the concept of earthly, localized kingdoms—"nations"[1]—we start to see how confessing is vital to accessing the means of Christ's grace as a society.

Lastly, the "end." The end is a total victory of Jesus' campaign, "all nations." Both Joshua's and Jesus' commissions are land campaigns. There is also a link to Adam's land campaign. G. K. Beale shows how the whole-earth concept is the *telos* from the very beginning. He writes, "Notice that Jesus uses the same divine accompaniment formula that God used in the later applications and reiteration of Adam's commission to the patriarchs and Israel to subdue and rule over the earth."[2] He says that now Christ, working through His people, will accomplish what Adam, Noah, and Israel failed to carry out.

We said earlier that our strategy is dependent on where things are on a timeline. Strategy, once again, is the estimation and practice of causation, and causation relates to timing. Notice the timing here. In both commissions, Joshua's and the Great one, the charge to keep all the commandments was not something that came at the end of the conquest for God's people. It was part of the conquest. It was one of the "ways" to keep their way prosperous and have good success (Josh. 1:8).

I am not saying that the only way to look at the Great Commission is through a strategic or a confessionalism lens. There are other ways to look at it. To me, however, it is remarkably similar to a "MISSION STATEMENT" I would read in a four-star's campaign plan. When we see comprehensiveness and confessionalism as ways—rather than ends—in the Great Commission, they become more actionable. They are earlier on the strategy timeline.

City on a Hill

Politicians are always calling for unity. We need unity in the church, but we need *antithesis* in the world. By antithesis, we show what is good and bad, beautiful and ugly, lawful and unlawful. Paradoxically, by accentuating antithesis we can reduce antithesis over time. That is what the City on a Hill is all about.

C. S. Lewis wrote, "Good is always getting better and bad is always getting worse: the possibilities of even apparent neutrality are always diminishing."[3] Lewis' statement is one of good and bad. One good thing is that by the divergence of good and bad, we can tell the difference. We are not glad that the valleys are getting lower, but we are happy to see any hill rising higher because it enlarges the antithesis. This antithesis will cause God-ordained jealousy as the cities in the valley cannot compete (Deut. 28:10).

The City on a Hill brings forward those maxims we mentioned earlier, Jesus' mediatorial reign, comprehensiveness, and confessionalism in a complete package. That makes the "city" *distinct* and enables it to be used as a way of Kingdom realization. The principle behind the City on a Hill is that obedience to God is attractive. This attractiveness glorifies God, and it spurs people on to inquiry. Therefore things such as pure worship, beauty, and culture can also be ways of Kingdom realization. It is not that these elements are salvific, but they are still causal. God uses them to achieve proper jealousy. John Winthrop put the idea into operation with his famous statement, "For we must consider that we shall be as a city upon a hill; the eyes of all the people are upon us."[4]

If Plymouth, as a little settlement across a vast ocean, had the eyes of all the world on it, surely a good number of specific counties in the US can achieve the same sort of God-given influence.

First-Mover Advantage

Militaries and businesses alike use the term First-Mover Advantage (FMA). God built into nature that the one pressing the attack has the advantage. Any professional tennis player who wins the toss will elect to serve because statistically, the server gains more points.

So who is making the first moves today, us or the secularists? Stop and think a minute about your favorite conservative podcast or news program. What are they discussing? What topic is their "special guest" talking about on any given day? I have found that such podcasts and programs are almost always reporting on what the secularists are doing in society. The typical podcast is predictable:
- Report about what the enemy has done.
- Say why it is wrong biblically.
- Give an exhortation to stop this from happening.
- Sign off saying, "See ya next week."

I'm exaggerating a bit, but if we take a hard look, we'll see we as Christians are mostly reactive. Most Christian podcasts and blogs would self-implode if the secularists stopped their activity. There would be nothing left to talk about.

Overall, our strategy of cultural engagement has been to *win by not losing*. We can't win that way. Even if we take action on every bad thing that the secularists do, the most we can do is maintain ground. Even our battle against abortion is defensive. We are trying to prevent institutionalized murder, and we are trying to get back to 1972. That does not mean we should not defend the fatherless (obviously). Abortion is an atrocious sin, and God wants us to fight back. Fighting back in some sense is offensive because His Word does not return void. What I am saying is that our strategy needs to be overall offensive for heaven's ethics to invade earth.

The Great Commission and the City on a Hill are not reactive. Both of them have a positive, gracious, causal element to them. Likewise, we should not be reactive. Neither should we be neutral if we expect to reverse the cultural trend. Jesus' authority enables and encourages us to seize the First-Mover Advantage. The question we should be asking is: how can we get out of reactive mode societally?

The Third Offset

One way to get out of reactive mode is to "offset." In 2014, the US military implemented a new strategy. We called it the "Third Offset." It wasn't completely new; there were two other offsets before this one (hence the name). We borrowed the term "offset" from the tactics of aerial attacks. In a strategic sense, we offset by purposely ignoring our enemy for a while in order to *build instead of react.*

The First Offset was in the 1950s with President Eisenhower. Rather than respond to the conventional weapons buildup of the Warsaw Pact in Eastern Europe, Eisenhower built a nuclear response plan. Many of his advisors were pushing for a better tank than the Russians (and deploying lots of them), but Eisenhower went nuclear. The Russians were stumped. They could not compete with this approach. Today strategists generally agree that Eisenhower won this Cold War standoff in more ways than one.

The Second Offset was from 1975 to 1989. A portion of the military ignored the world for a bit and developed things like stealth, GPS, precision-guided weapons, and datalinks.

As mentioned, the Third Offset started in 2014, and we are still in this one. This one is about unmanned aerial vehicles, undersea water vehicles, miniaturization, improvement of space communication, and now, cyber.

In these offsets, we realized that in order to get ahead of the enemy, we needed to tell a segment of our military to pretend the enemy was not there. We did not react to our enemies; we leapfrogged them. And it worked. When our adversaries got to the next decade, we were waiting for them. Offsets are one of the primary ways the US has maintained the advantage. Our enemies have been reacting to us, trying to catch up to us for seventy years now.[5]

The Great Commission is strategy par excellence. It has a power source (Christ), ways (comprehensiveness and confessing Christ), and ends (total victory over the earth). The City on a Hill is a good sub-strategy, conveying two essential elements: distinction and timing. The City, if it is distinct from the broader culture, leverages jealousy as a good thing. It glorifies God and leads people to inquire and find out more about this unknown God (Acts 17:23). But we should not put this off to the future. We may have missed the fact that the City exists in our current history as a causal element. If we relegate the City on the Hill to the end of the gospel campaign, we miss the whole point of it.

Like Piper taught us, anytime we can move things from the future to the present and make them actionable, we improve our strategy. We said the confessional county strategy would move several elements from an "end" to a "way." Those elements we seek to move forward are Christ's current, mediatorial reign, the comprehensiveness of Christian culture, and confessionalism. In the rest of the book, we will also speak of culture, beauty, worship, localism and the Christian settlement as other "ways."

Building rather than reforming is something Dreher recommended in his book, and I agree with him. Taking the initiative is risky but is sometimes necessary. The Russians would not dare do an offset strategy because they do not have the resources to take the technological high ground. President Reagan leveraged this with "Star Wars" missile defense and convinced the Soviets to reduce their nuclear stockpile. The point is that the side with the greater resources is the one who can do offset strategies effectively. Since we have the greatest Resource in the universe, perhaps we should "offset" and build culture rather than react to it. Doing so may shake things up a bit.

CULTURE, BEAUTY AND WORSHIP AS A "WAY"

We are far too easily pleased.[1]
C.S. LEWIS

I n his book *You Are What You Love*, James K. A. Smith depicts culture in terms of liturgy. Not just the liturgy you have on Sunday mornings, but liturgy throughout everyday life. He writes, "Liturgies, then, are calibration technologies. They train our loves by aiming them toward a certain *telos*."[2] The reason culture trains our heart is that, in a sense, it is a type of liturgy.

I think Smith is onto something with his liturgy theme. The Bible says our hearts can be turned. Of those who would not obey Moses in the Exodus, the Bible says, "in their hearts [they] turned back again into Egypt" (Acts 7:39). Their affections turned back to the *culture* of Egypt, not actual Egypt, and they said to Aaron, "Up, make us gods, which shall go before us; for as for this Moses, the man that brought us up out of the land of Egypt, we wot not what is become of him" (Ex. 32:1).

Smith is right about this: "You can't not love."[3] We will love something. Our ever-loving-something hearts can be trained, for better or worse, by the liturgy that is our culture. We would like to believe that the people of God are only trained by the Bible, but we need to admit we are also trained by culture. God admitted it. He knows our weakness. When the Israelites were first crossing the Jordon and God ordered them to "utterly destroy" everyone, it was not so they could inherit the land unencumbered. Rather, God determined that total annihilation of the pagan culture was the only way that the Israelites could remain holy. Removing the pagans was imperative because of their negative *cultural* influence. We read:

> For they will turn away thy son from following me, that they may serve other gods: so will the anger of the LORD be kindled against you, and destroy thee suddenly. But thus shall ye deal with them; ye shall destroy their altars, and break down their images, and cut down their groves, and burn their graven images with fire. For thou art an holy people unto the LORD thy God: the LORD thy God hath chosen thee to be a special people unto himself, above all people that are upon the face of the earth. (Deuteronomy 7:4-6)

Of course, God is not telling us to reset the culture by destroying people today. We have no such mandate. Our weapon is the gracious Sword of the Spirit. But this passage shows that even as God's people seek to change the culture they live in, *they are inescapably affected by it*, especially over the long haul.

The Pilgrims admitted the influence of culture. They packed up again and left after being in Holland for eleven years. The familiar story is that the Puritans came to America because of religious persecution. That is not entirely true. They *came to Holland* because of religious persecution, but they came *to America* for several reasons, and all of them had to do with a long-term vision for their prodigy and advancement of the Kingdom. The culture in Holland was not good. Cotton Mather wrote:

> They saw, that whatever banks the Dutch had against the inroads of the sea, they had not sufficient ones against a flood of manifold profaneness. They could not with ten years' endeavor bring their neighbors particularly to any suitable observation of the LORD'S DAY; without which they knew that all practical Religion must wither miserably. They beheld some of their children, by the temptations of the place, which were especially given in the licentious ways of many young people, drawn into dangerous extravagancies.[4]

Mather's point brings up a question for us today: Do we have "banks" sufficient to hold back the manifold profaneness of our culture? What would the Pilgrims do in our culture? At least the Dutch knew there was a "Lord's Day." Our culture is undoubtedly worse than the one the Pilgrims left.

Based on their actions and their writing, if the Pilgrims were our consultants today, I think they would put it back in our lap. They would probably say, "If you can hold back the culture's influence long enough so that you can change it before it changes your children, you should stay. If not, you have no choice but to make some sort of change. You would be better off to find a way to create culture from the bottom up as much as possible." Culture was important to the Pilgrims. This wasn't every Christian's mindset in 1620, but it seems to have been theirs.

A Culture of Beauty

Jealousy is good when we are making people desire the good things of God. "Let *your* light so shine before men, that they may see *your* good works, and glorify *your Father* which is in heaven" (Matt. 5:16, emphasis added). Comprehensive Christianity does this. It makes the nations jealous. You put all these God-ordained institutions, covenanted with Christ, in one geophysical area, and you are set to let the light shine because God designed it that way. It may not happen right away, and it may not be easy, but we have to believe what the Bible says. In the midst of the famous chapter on blessings, Deuteronomy 28, we see this important verse:

> And all people of the earth shall see that thou art called by the name of the LORD; and they shall be afraid of thee. (Deuteronomy 28:10)

The Huguenots made nations jealous with their beautiful culture. They created their own subculture as a minority people, and their reputation was excellent.[5] Their beauty was preceded only by their holiness. They lived the good life as much as possible. William Henry Foote in his wonderful book on the Huguenots writes, "Men and women were taught to expect their highest earthly enjoyments in the domestic relations."[6] Foote says you could always tell what areas the Huguenots lived in: "The vine-clad hills and fertile vales were the abodes of simple-hearted cheerfulness and piety."[7]

They were also the best at their trades and were astute thinkers. Another author writes of them, "the higher the status of the artisan, the more likely he was a Protestant; the more literate and self-confident, the more likely to reject the tutelage of the clergy and to take the idea of the priesthood of all believers."[8] In short, it was hard not to respect their people and their culture. King Louis said, "They are better Christians than we are."[9]

I am not saying that beauty will keep a culture righteous. Some of the most beautiful locations are now spiritually dead. When I was in Fairford, England I enjoyed frequenting the "Bull" pub and hotel. It was beautiful, and you could smell the history. After a beer, it seems you just had to pull out your pipe and walk around the town square. When I walked up to the 300-year-old church in the middle of town, I saw some flyers on the door. They were not advertising a preaching series, Bible studies, or a psalm sing. Instead, they were advertising community events that could hardly be distinguished from a humanist club meeting. Beauty here was external only.

Beauty will not keep a culture righteous, but we should not blame beauty for culture's decrepitude. It was not beauty's fault. The externalism came not because the outside lived but because the inside died. It was a loss of their first love, of Jesus and His precious Word. There is a lesson here we must learn. God has shown us that in the next Christendom, we should keep our Bibles handy and trust them.

But we need beauty. If beauty is not part of our strategy, we lose the ability to appreciate and enjoy the beauty of the Lord. God has not given us a beauty timeout, a parenthesis on the beauty timeline, somewhere between Aaron's holy garments (Ex. 28:2) and the New Jerusalem with its jasper stone, clear as crystal (Rev. 21:11). Rather, we should see beauty as something that strings generations together. We should build things made to last generations and that are objectively beautiful.

Protestant Medievalism and Agrarianism

Any discussion on culture today has to include a discussion on technology. You should probably put down this book and go read chapter eleven of *Angels in the Architecture* by Douglas Jones and Douglas Wilson. Jones and Wilson show that while medievalism is not to be adulated as some grand golden age, it had a harmonious culture worth admiring. Medievalism had tangible Christianity and a life more in line with the pace of Hebraic family and community life. Jones and Wilson call it "Protestant Medievalism" by which they mean medievalism with a good splash of Reformed theology.

Modernity, the antagonist of medievalism, is not all bad, however. It has some wonderful benefits. Wilson writes, "Three cheers for central heating, antibiotics, and all of that."[10] To eschew these heavenly gifts would be to exasperate our wives and children, not to mention offensive to the Father who gave them. To shun technology would be to cut off our own thumbs in the clubbing-fight for our culture.

Medieval culture is indeed set on the opposite side of modernity, and the challenge is to pick from both baskets without falling into either. Jones' and Wilson's solution is to *harmonize* technology, harmonize it with a day-to-day lifestyle of home and hearth and society. First, have a "profound gratitude" for technology. Actually thank God for refrigeration and your computer. Second, do not buy into the scientism of technology that says our lives depend on it. Recognize that man has built, and continues to build, many towers of Babel. Some approaches to technology can be like that. Third, use it for the Kingdom, carefully:

> A man may accept some of the fruits of modernity in order to spur himself on in the work of building a medieval culture. But he must be careful to teach his sons.[11]

That last sentence will be the most challenging. The authors are saying that technology can be used, but teach your sons how to handle that dragon. This book was written in 1998, before social media. Most people communicated by landline and maybe dial-up internet. Today, we are even more entrenched in modernity, industrialism, and technocratism.

I believe that Jones' and Wilson's vision of Protestant Medievalism is attainable for this reason: the basic patterns of life that God gave us will not cease. We still need homes and ways to communicate and food (which means we need topsoil). Paul said to be content with clothing and food. That does not mean we should strive to have those things *only*. Asceticism and Luddism[12] are simply not biblical. Paul's statement to be content with basic needs means that there is a baseline to which we can add selectively, choosing technology that will enhance our lives and Kingdom effectiveness without ungodly generational trappings.

Worship as a Way

Worship, like the other strategic components in this book, is a "way" of Kingdom realization, not a result of it. It is true there will be greater, more pure worship in eternity, and we should look forward to that. But even now, the angels are proclaiming the glories of Jesus (Rev. 5:11-12).

Joshua's army is an excellent example of worship being a "way." After crossing the Jordon, the first thing they did was circumcise all the men (Josh. 5:3). How foolish this seems to the unregenerate mind. To purposely put the survival of the entire nation at risk makes no earthly sense. Yet they wanted to approach God in worship in their new homeland. When they circumcised themselves, they could not trust in chariots and men but only in God for protection.

Ezra's assembly, upon returning from exile, also showed that worship is a way of Kingdom realization. The mission of the returning exiles was to build the temple. But they didn't wait for the temple to be built to worship. As soon as they had houses to live in (Ezra 2:70), the people gathered for worship, and they built an altar to the Lord (3:1-3). The interesting thing is that, even though they were in enemy territory, they didn't hide the fact they were going to restore worship. They put the altar smack-dab where the old one used to be.[13] And here's the reason: "for fear was upon them because of the people of those coun-tries" (3:3). Interpretations of this "fear" vary, but I take it to mean they knew they needed God's help. Whatever the case, they did not delay worship, and they did not go underground.

Both Joshua and Ezra demonstrated the necessity of feasting, which is a form of worship. After Joshua's men healed from the circumcision, the next order of business was to keep the Passover *in the plains of Jericho*. This was a terrible position militarily. The plains afford virtually no geographic defense, especially if hemmed in on one side by a river. Yet unleavened cakes were baked, parched corn consumed. At the culmination of these events, they get a special appearance by the pre-incarnate Christ, "captain of the host of the LORD am I now come" (Josh. 5:14), showing that feasting is fighting more than resting (though it is both because Jesus has already won). Ezra's band, after building the altar amid their enemies, kept the Feast of Booths, once again in a very visible and vulnerable position.

You see, Joshua and Ezra were on the winning side. I can think of nothing more bold and confident than to sit down for a nice meal right in front of your enemies. It shows the enemy he is weaker. When we feast today at the Lord's Table, we are fighting and realizing the Kingdom every time. "For as often as ye eat this bread and drink this cup, ye do shew the Lord's death till he come" (1 Cor. 11:26).

Imagine how our enemies, the principalities and rulers of darkness, feel when we feast and declare victory. Clausewitz gives some insight (humanly speaking) of what it feels like to be on the losing side. He gives a soul-stirring account of a man becoming gradually aware of his impending defeat. What starts as a question in an officer's mind winds up being an unwelcome fact in his whole body. A retreat is ordered, and stragglers are left behind in the confusion. Such is the condition of demons. Clausewitz writes,

> What is worse, the sense of being beaten is not a mere nightmare that may pass; it has become a palpable fact that the enemy is stronger.[14]

And so God's and our enemies get a gut-punch when we worship in Spirit and in truth.

Both Joshua and Ezra show the claiming of territory by worship, and territory-claiming worship shows up elsewhere in the Bible. Using Malachi 1:11, Calvin shows that thank offerings today are the new covenant equivalent of old covenant incense. The practice of thank offerings has nothing to with appeasing God's wrath, obtaining forgiveness for sins, or meriting righteousness, "but is concerned solely with magnifying and exalting God."[15] What is interesting is the geographical nature of the incense of the old covenant (and, by extension, the thank offerings of the new). Notice what Malachi 1:11 says:

> For from the rising of the sun even unto the going down of the same my name shall be great among the Gentiles; and *in every place incense shall be offered unto my name,* and a pure offering: for my name shall be great among the heathen, saith the LORD of hosts. (emphasis added)

Even a thank offering places a guidon in the ground for Christ. There is so much that is done locally with worship. When souls are re-created salvifically,[16] that happens in a particular household, in a particular town, and often in a particular church. It is by faith that we conquer kingdoms (Heb. 11:33). And kingdoms are territorial. Even casting out demons is territorial. Demons are not omnipresent and can be forced out of geographical areas (Matt. 8:28; Mark 5:10; Luke 11:24; Rev. 9:14). Worship is a way to gain some (literal) ground for Jesus.

Christian culture is not something that happens at the end. It happens along the way. Christian culture is putting God's ethics into public action. That is what we are praying for when we pray *God's will be done on earth, as it is in heaven.* If James Smith's book was correct about our hearts being trained by love and our love being framed by the liturgy of culture, maybe we should evaluate whether our children can hold back the influence of culture long enough for us to change it. If not, maybe it is time to take measures to get to a place to create culture.

If we do that, we have some good historical examples. Creating a beautiful culture in Huguenot fashion that points our hearts to God and helps us enjoy earthly and heavenly gifts is a great strategy. It makes the nations jealous and therefore has a double benefit.

Technology is not all bad, but neither is medievalism or agrarianism. It may be time to take a fresh look at the cultural influences of technology to determine where it is helping and where it is hurting on our path toward Christ-likeness.

And finally, worship, to include feasting, makes territorial claims for Christ. We are to worship the Lord in the beauty of holiness (Ps. 96:9), exercising a *way* of Kingdom realization in our time. According to Scripture, this is something we can do, something we can "work" at:

> And let the beauty of the LORD our God be upon us: and establish thou the work of our hands upon us; yea, the *work of our hands* establish thou it. (Psalm 90:17, emphasis added)

11

LOCALISM AS A "WAY"

Not long ago, a friend of mine called me up as a witness that indeed the world was round, not flat. I used to fly U-2s, and we flew at altitudes high enough to see the curvature of the earth. I can say firsthand that the "flat-earth conspiracy" is not true. My readers may already know this. I have pictures to prove it just in case there is any doubt.

But Thomas Friedman thinks the earth is flat. He wrote a book, *The World is Flat*. He thinks the world is flat because of *globalization*. Friedman was the leading spokesman for the idea that the world is interconnected now as never before. He takes us on a historical tour and shows us "Ten Forces that Flattened the World." The first "force" was the Berlin wall coming down. This event made us think about the world and "to see it as a seamless whole."[1] When the wall came down, global opportunities went up. The tenth and last force came in various forms of technology. Friedman called these technologies "steroids" because they made us go faster and do more.[2]

None of us would dispute; the world is more interconnected now than a hundred years ago. I doubt, however, it is more interconnected than in the first few centuries of the gospel's breakthrough. And I submit we should not passively concede everything to globalism. We should distinguish between what is shared and what is not. For example, information is shared globally, and Chinese electronic components are shared globally. But most of our laws are local.

Upon closer analysis, we see that most of our interactions with people are local. The most important thing we do our whole lives, worship God, is done locally. Worship is not really worship without localism. A globalized church with online services is still forsaking the assembly (Heb. 10:25), no matter how digitally connected it might be.

I do not deny globalism. The world is very connected. But globalism has not replaced localism, and it never will. You still need the stocker and the checker at Walmart to sell you that Chinese coffee maker, and you still need a local internet service provider with local copper (or fiberoptic) wires to connect you to the world. The fact is, you cannot have globalism without localism.

Land-based Covenants

All of God's covenants are connected to the land in one way or another, and these covenants act as the glue for localism. God gave man stewardship over the Garden of Eden (Gen. 2:15), a pilot project to take care of the land. He renewed the covenant with Noah (Gen. 9:1), and again it involved the earth with a natural sign—the rainbow (Gen. 9:13). God guaranteed Abraham a specific portion of the earth (Gen. 17:8), promising the whole earth to his descendants by faith (Gen. 22:18). The covenant with Moses gave Israel the Promised Land (Ex. 6:4). God renewed the land promise in the "little commission" to Joshua (Josh. 1:2-3), and the new covenant shows Jesus expanding the idea in the Sermon on the Mount (Matt. 5:5). We see the same concept in the Lord's Prayer and the Great Commission.

From beginning to end, God's covenants are connected to the land. Rushdoony says, "A neglected aspect of the Bible is that God's covenant with man is land-based."[3] He explains that the land, because it is coupled to covenants, is *either blessed or cursed*. But one thing that Rushdoony does not bring out is the local element of land curses. He sees the "land" as the whole earth. He emphasizes, for example, that Joshua's conquest of Canaan is a type of Jesus' conquest of the entire world. This is true; the whole earth is the *telos* of the gospel. But in his lecture series titled "The Theology of the Land," Rushdoony does not mention anything about God's interaction with localities. Old Testament history has many aspects, but one of them is a story of *different, local* lands.

And the local, land-based element is not abated in the New Testament. The Hebraic mindset of the New Testament is different from ours. When we read "earth," we typically visualize photographs shot from the Apollo space missions. We see a beautiful blue and white sphere, prettier than any bowling ball ever built. But the Hebraic mind had not even been airborne, much less gone into orbit. When Jesus says, "Blessed are the meek: for they shall inherit the earth" (Matt. 5:5), we should consider that the Greek word for "earth" is γῆ, which means earth, soil, or the surface of the earth. It is the same word we see in the Lord's Prayer, "on γῆ as it is in heaven." Terra firma is more in mind here.

This is confirmed by Psalm 37:11, from which Jesus pulls. Psalm 37 speaks of the fact that the wicked shall be soon cut off, and His people shall dwell in the land (v. 3). The tenor of Psalm 37 is more local than global.

Even the Great Commission presupposed localism. We think of the *whole earth* with the Great Commission, and we think rightly. But the fact that we have to "go" means you can't do this remotely. You cannot stay in California and fly your drone overseas and drop gospel bombs on Afghanistan. You have to put boots on the ground locally. Jesus' ministry was local, from town to town, and so was Paul's. Both of them worked in the context of towns and regions. We fulfill the global Great Commission in a local "way" that will eventually convert the world.

We saw in chapter three that land curses are geographic. God curses or blesses a region and the people that live there. Let's look at another example from Deuteronomy chapter 21. A dead body is discovered out in the country, and no one knows who killed the man (v. 1). The first thing the elders and judges of the surrounding cities need to do is get out their measuring instruments to determine which city is closest to the body (v. 2). That is important because the closest town is responsible for handling this matter.

The elders of that city have to sacrifice a heifer in place of the murderer. (Of course, this heifer does not completely replace the murderer. If the murderer is found, he will still have to die.) The land is defiled, and through the heifer the Lord provides a way for the land to be cleansed. This must be done because God dwells among His people, and yet He will not remain in a land guilty of bloodshed (Num. 35:34).

So the town closest to the murder has to sacrifice a

heifer, but then they also have to confess as a society. Deuteronomy 21:5-8 says:

> And the priests the sons of Levi shall come near; . . . And all the elders of that city, that are next unto the slain man, shall wash their hands over the heifer that is beheaded in the valley: and they shall answer and say, Our hands have not shed this blood, neither have our eyes seen it. Be merciful, O LORD, unto thy people Israel, whom thou hast redeemed, and lay not innocent blood unto thy people of Israel's charge. And the blood shall be forgiven them.

Notice once again, we have representative heads of all-of-society. The local elders (civil leaders) and the local sons of Levi (the church) have to confess.[4] Yet another example of social confessionalism.

Today, when we hear about a dead body in the field around a town, our primary concern is finding the murderer. While important, that does not seem to be the main concern of the Bible. The primary concern is how to cleanse the land locally so that God's presence is not hindered.

What Is Wrong (and Right) with the City?

Since we are speaking of localism, we should discuss urban and rural localities. In the 2020 presidential election, every major metropolitan area voted for Biden except Greenville, South Carolina. With elections, the biggest split is not among regions or states but between the cities and the country. Look at an election map and you will see what I mean. It is binary: cities are blue, rural areas are red. This is true even for California and New York. Of course, whether a county is red or blue does not determine righteousness, but it shows an overall cultural difference.

The problem with the city is not the city itself. The Lord has a lot of good things to say about cities. The Father only gives good things (Matt. 7:11), and one thing He gives is cities (Deut. 19:7). Cities can be blessed just as much as the countryside (Deut. 28:3), and they can flourish: "There shall be an handful of corn in the earth upon the top of the mountains; the fruit thereof shall shake like Lebanon: and they of the city shall flourish like grass of the earth" (Ps. 72:16). God, after all, has His own city, and it is a happy place: "There is a river, the streams whereof shall make glad the city of God, the holy place of the tabernacles of the most High" (Ps. 46:4).

Cities are important. Without a doubt, cities are more influential than country towns. Jesus wanted Paul to preach at Jerusalem and at Rome (Acts 23:11). The early church strategically went into influential cities. It is usually the cities that turn tides in world history.

But there are challenges with the *modern city*. The modern city lacks accountability. Ancient cities had more accountability because they were more connected. That meant that the gospel was transmitted faster and more face-to-face. Jonah preached to Nineveh, a large city, and the whole city repented, including the king. Ancient cities did not have air-conditioned offices and homes and mobile capsules (automobiles) that could carry you from your garage to the other edge of the city without even looking at anyone, much less talking to them. With public transportation and the internal combustion engine and, of course, smartphones, interconnectedness with the world went up and with neighbors went down. See if anyone says hello the next time you are on a subway in Boston.

Also, today's cities do not have a prominent cultural center, a common touchpoint, whether it be the temple of God or the temple of Diana. Roland de Vaux writes in his book *Ancient Israel*, "Private citizens in Israel did business only in their own locality, in the town village or square, where the market was held (2 Kings 7:1)."[5] The cities of old had interconnectedness and accountability. You could not hide as easily, and that's a good check on the depravity of man.

If we could find a way to have local accountability in highly-populated cities, they would be more righteous. It is not impossible. Israel was able to do that with a large population of people marching out of Egypt. The communication flowed very quickly, and accountability was almost immediate. Using the structure of tribes, families, and households, Joshua pinpointed Achan and his sin in a single day (Josh. 7:14-22).[6] There are other examples. The New Testament shows the whole city of Jerusalem was in an uproar over Jesus. Paul preached to "almost the whole city" of Antioch (Acts 13:44). Later, the whole city of Jerusalem tried to kill Paul before the centurion saved him (Acts 21:31-33). The ancient cities were more interconnected, which means they had more accountability.

A related topic is accessibility to rulers. The Bible assumes normal people will be connected to the local rulers. It is not just a small, elite segment of society who rubs elbows with rulers. Notice that Proverbs 23:1 assumes you will eat with your rulers: "When thou sittest to eat with a ruler, consider diligently what is before thee." Personally, I have lived in the city, and I have lived in a small, rural town. I cannot remember ever speaking to a leader in the city, but I have talked to almost all our local leaders within two years of moving to my rural town. Results may vary. But fundamentally, rural areas will have more access to rulers because everyone shares the same gathering points. I call this "grocery-store accountability," and I believe it is very important to have.

The modern city is also more separated from creation and the natural environment. If the heavens declare the glory of God and convict people of sin (Ps. 19), what if the view of the heavens and the stars is obstructed by buildings and city lights? Stories abound of the first time an inner-city kid went camping and saw the stars. Rushdoony says a lack of experience in natural creation leads to dualism, separation of the creation from the Creator.[7] It is true you can still have a garden in the city and be connected to creation. But ancient cities were more in touch with creation as a whole.

The biggest challenge with the modern city is its pluralism and public idolatry. Modern cities are structured today to encourage and even celebrate pluralism. Global corporations and universities strive for diversity. As we saw earlier in such passages as Deuteronomy 13, public practice of unbiblical religion (which today would be mosques, Buddhist temples, Roman Catholic churches, etc.) is idolatry and puts the city under God's condemnation.[8] Pluralism (which results in publicly-practiced idolatry) must be removed for God to approve a geographical area for blessings (Ex. 23:24-33; Lev. 26:1, 4-6; Deut. 13:12-18; 17:1-7; Isa. 24:5).

This applies to any city or town, urban or rural. So this is not just an urban problem. God will eventually remove all idolatry. There are, however, some small towns with no idolatrous churches. Even if a small town does have a single Roman Catholic church (most have one), it will be easier to get rid of than multiple ones in a city (plus all the mosques, etc.). The question is not whether God will do that. He will remove all idolatry. The question I think we should ask is, how long will it take?[9] Of course, there is no divine command to leave a city that has institutionalized idolatry. It is not sinful to stay in that city (or in a rural town). God is pleased with people who are trying to claim the city for Christ. If all Christians leave cities, the remnant protection is gone. And what about the unbelievers? How shall they hear without a preacher? I am just calling attention to the Bible's view that idolatry causes a geographic land curse.[10]

In my opinion, Douglas Jones gives a reasonable view of the modern city. He acknowledges the city is presented in positive terms in the Bible and that cities are very influential. The trajectory, writes Jones, is *toward the city*. The path from Genesis to Revelation is the path of garden to city.[11] Yet he is concerned (as I am) about the long-term impact the city's culture will have on our children. Our environment affects us more than we know. The future city, says Jones, will absorb some of the qualities of the country. He concludes, "the faithful city of the future will resemble the country far more than it does any modern city."[12]

I wonder if it is not possible to start a new city. It must be. All the cities we have now were started at some point by some people.

Resistance and the Lesser Magistrate

Another important aspect of localism deals with resisting tyranny. In late 2020 and early 2021, Christian books about resistance were flying off the presses. COVID-19 was our wake-up call, and we seemed to be at least rubbing our eyes and getting out of bed (metaphorically speaking).

I am thankful for these new books on resistance. I am grateful most of them are pulling from old authors, brilliant and faithful men such as Samuel Rutherford, Du-Plessis-Mornay, and Pierre Viret. Each book deals with various aspects of resistance against unbiblical authority, but one aspect that is very important doctrinally is *who* should do the resisting. Who should do the resisting?

Normally, even the church should not have to represent itself against tyranny. I am thankful for the churches that stood up during COVID and continued to worship in defiance of laws that disregard biblical parameters for quarantine. But actually, local magistrates should have been the first to resist the tyrannical COVID measures. There is no authority except from God (Rom. 13:1), and He ordained different roles for each jurisdiction. God appointed the *civil magistrate* for good (Rom. 13:4), so that office should be the first to resist unrighteous laws. The old authors did not have to address this as much because it was well known. Christendom was more decentralized than our current society; their lives were more connected to local, lesser magistrates. And those local, lesser magistrates were connected to the church.

I think Matt Trewhella's 2013 book, *The Doctrine of the Lesser Magistrate,* will remain one of the most, if not the most, important book to read on this subject going forward. Trewhella makes a solid case for biblical interposition—within the civil jurisdiction—by pulling from John Knox's *Appellation*. Trewhella's book describes how Daniel and his cohorts, *as leaders*, stood up against Nebuchadnezzar's laws. He points out their stand was "theocentric."[13] It was their knowledge of God's law and their commitment to it that made their disobedience approved (and effective). Trewhella presents the negative example from Jeremiah 36:9-31. King Jehoiakim's lesser magistrates (princes) gave a half-hearted attempt at interposition when the king cut and burned Jeremiah's prophecy. Jehoiakim had his own plans—to fight Babylon—and Jeremiah was getting in the way. He had Jeremiah and his scribe arrested while the princes did nothing. As Jehoiakim's negative example shows us, the lesser magistrate can influence whether a county is blessed or cursed. A failure to interpose can not only mean loss of freedom; it can mean generational punishment for the whole area (Jer. 36:31). Tyranny is bad enough, but God can also punish us for allowing tyranny.

In addition to their lawful, God-given authority, the lesser magistrates have some practical advantages. They have an established base of popular support, and constitutional law is usually on their side. Trewhella writes, "Lesser magistrates have the best chance of resolving injustice without upheaval or bloodshed. A tyrannical government is less anxious to push their opposition if they know that the opposition has the proper leadership and order of lesser magistrates."[14]

The doctrine of the lesser magistrate makes achieving the confessional county even more appealing. Resistance needs to be based on a three-way covenant (as Rutherford reminds us in *Lex Rex*) between God, the civil magistrate, and the people.[15] This approach lines up perfectly with social confessionalism. We mentioned earlier that cities are very influential. But with a unified population and a biblical lesser magistrate, a rural country town can also make a difference. The story of the Reformation is a story of country towns converting, one by one. As Trewhella explains, the town of Magdeburg saved the Reformation by its winsome, confessional stance against King Charles V.[16]

Impending Decentralization

The antifederalists may ultimately be proven right. They said the US is too large and too diverse to stay together for the long term. The "indivisible" in our pledge of allegiance is more and more being called into question.

Colin Woodard, in his book *American Nation: A History of the Eleven Rival Regional Cultures of North America,* says much the same. Woodard may not be coming at this from our worldview, but he can see the difference a worldview makes. Writing in 2011, he is surprisingly prescient:

> In the midst of, say, a deadly pandemic outbreak or the destruction of several cities by terrorists, a fearful public might condone suspension of civil rights, the dissolution of Congress, or the incarceration of Supreme Court justices. One can easily imagine circumstances in which some nations are happy with the new order and others deeply opposed to it. [Woodard sees eleven cultural "nations" in the US]. With the constitution abandoned, the federation could well disintegrate, forming one or more confederations of like-minded regions.[17]

The COVID-19 pandemic has divided the nation with a sharp cleaver. It has also (on the good side) been a tremendous intelligence-gathering event for us. We can see which states uphold "safety first" and which states are more concerned about freedom and jurisdictional lines. To put it another way, we can see which states see safety as an individual choice and which states see it as a policy prerogative.

The most important civics lesson in COVID was the fact that *each state chose for itself.* We should not miss this. Each state chose its own response. This is important for two reasons. First, we see that constitutionally, it still matters which powers are enumerated and which ones are not. This pesky constitution of ours may have gotten in the way of President Trump, and it certainly gets in the way of President Biden. When asked if he would issue a nationwide mask mandate, Biden replied that he couldn't. He knew he did not have the authority, but it was apparent he wanted a mandate.

Second, COVID-19 shows that Woodard was right. America does have regional cultures, and Americans do want self-rule. We saw a hint of Woodard's "confederation of like-minded regions" in the disputed 2020 election. On December 8, 2020, Texas Attorney General Ken Paxton filed a lawsuit to contest the administration of the 2020 election. Texas hit a beehive (or maybe it created one). A "coalition" of twenty-one "law-abiding" states joined in the lawsuit.[18] Most states were making a point, showing which side they were on. This was unusual. We often see people and political parties making stands, but states haven't made a significant stand like this in a long time. There are many ways to label 2020, but I submit one of them might be, "The Year of the State."

Not only is there a resurgence of state sovereignty, but counties are beginning to feel their oats. The "sanctuary county" concept was originally created for liberal counties to push back against President Trump's anti-immigration policies. One wonders if they knew they were borrowing from Christian doctrine when they attempted to exercise interposition. As it turns out, the conservatives co-opted the idea, and now we have "constitutional counties" and "sanctuary counties for the unborn." Most of these counties have made resolutions, with county leaders in session, that they intend to uphold the biblical rights of the unborn and the constitutional right to arm themselves. As Paul Michael Raymond said recently, what we need now are Christian counties.[19]

Globalism cannot usurp localism. If we understand the land-based element of God's covenants, and especially if we exercise the three-way covenantal approach to government that Rutherford pointed to, we are on a path towards more local sovereignty. We have not even touched other elements such as decentralization's doomsday weapon: cryptocurrency.

Even though localism is on the rise—*perhaps because localism is on the rise*—the lesser magistrate will become more active in interposing against centralist governments as these central governments begin to lose grip. In my estimate, homeschooling will once again become a fighting ground like it was in the 1990s. In May 2020, *Harvard Magazine* published a provocative article titled, "The Risks of Homeschooling." In it, Elizabeth Bartholet, Wasserstein professor of law at the Law School's Child Advocacy Program, recommended a presumptive ban on homeschooling. She made the "discovery" that upwards of 90 percent of homeschoolers are Christians who want to remove their children from mainstream culture. Some of those parents are "extreme religious ideologues."[20] One wonders by what standard she is judging.

This issue faded into the background when COVID got hot, but we "extreme religious ideologues" have been identified. It is wonderful that COVID moved so many families to homeschool, but we should be ready for the blowback. This is just one example of how land-based localism and confessionalism are becoming more important.

Localism can be a "way" of Kingdom realization if we see it in a biblical way, in terms of land-based covenants. Jesus is our commander in His land campaign to take the world geographically. Particularly in rural areas, we can have *grocery-store accountability* and a connected small civilization. This allows us to say, "not in my town" a bit easier and to resist tyranny through our local magistrate. But mostly, biblical localism allows us to have ownership and build by His grace. May *our* land yield her increase:

> Truth shall spring out of the earth;
> and righteousness shall look down from heaven.
> Yea, the LORD shall give that which is good;
> and *our* land shall yield her increase.
> (Psalm 85:11-12, emphasis added)

12

REVIVING THE CHRISTIAN SETTLEMENT

No one should fear to undertake any task in the name of
our Savior, if it is just and if the intention is purely for His
holy service.
CHRISTOPHER COLUMBUS

Somewhere along the way, we lost the idea of new,
deliberate settlements. I mean, we *lost it*. Just drive
around the country. When was the last time you came into
a town that said something like, "Niceville, Ohio, est.
2019"? I am not talking about Chicago's latest bedroom
community that decided to incorporate and "establish"
themselves. I am talking about towns like Stanton, Iowa
(est. 1855), not far from my home, a place deliberately
chosen by Lutherans who had decided to start something
completely new. There was a nice high place to put a
church and build a community. They moved, and they
broke ground. The town is still beautiful and still going
strong.

The last big push for settlements was the Oklahoma

Sooners land rush in 1889. The US's last two settlements on the books are Las Vegas (1905) and Anchorage (1914).

I believe it is time to revive the practice of Christian settlements like we saw in the colonial era. By "Christian settlement," I mean colonies of heaven: deliberate, confessional mini-societies set up not to leave the world but to salt it up. If this sounds radical today, perhaps we have lost some of our ancestors' vision and theology. They had a different idea about packing up and moving. Rushdoony writes:

> They were emigrants and pilgrims, and America was their Promised Land. They looked confidently to the future therefore. It is a significant and melancholy fact that their descendants now look nostalgically to the past, a perspective not calculated to ensure victory.[1]

Notice what he says. Nostalgically relegating ventures of new civilization to the past is not a victorious perspective. Yet that is what we often do. We teach our children about the amazing risks our ancestors took and how it paid off. We tell them these were faithful actions by faithful families—things worthy of praise. And then we put the book back on the homeschooling shelf. I think we forget, sometimes, that the people who did those things were people like us, facing many of the same challenges. Their environment was remarkably similar to ours.

As I mentioned in the introduction, I am not saying everyone should become a settler. I am saying that some need to for the benefit of Christianity everywhere. Cotton Mather thought that a New England colony could impact the whole world. It was *their oblique maneuver*, their "City on a Hill." They were getting some maneuvering room away from the existing culture to establish a new, *distinct* one. I believe this is just as possible and just as needed today.

What Happened?

That the Western world stopped settlements and colonialism is one of the larger transitions in human history. There is a significant difference between starting new colonies and expanding existing ones. What stopped colonialism?

To answer that question, we should consider how it started. We are familiar in our circles with the religious impetus for early colonization. Yet economics also had a play in the early push. Even some of our favorite New England settlements were a mixture: some coming for religious reasons, some coming simply to improve their financial situation. In the agrarian societies of old, you looked for places you could raise your own food and make your own way. Of course, it was not just about individual choices or where to grow food. There were also empires wanting to establish themselves in the new world.[2] Once the expansion was complete in the early 1700s and we had a few wars to sort out the boundaries, empires sort of ran out of continents to claim.

Yet for North America, there was a lot more land to push into. "Go west, young man" was a didactic phrase, teaching a young man that risks taken early may pan out well in the long run. And so there was another push for settlements in the interior. But at some point, it stopped. Just by looking at the dates, the idea of Western settlements died a slow death starting in the War Between the

States. Some trickled on after the war, but the push was gone. That infamous war was undoubtedly a punishment for our refusal to repent of slavery and statism and (as we mentioned in the chapter on confessionalism) a refusal to acknowledge Jesus Christ as Lord. It would make sense that part of God's punishment would be to remove the practice of starting new towns and new opportunities.

What about more modern history? Why is the idea of deliberate settlements so foreign to the contemporary mind? Most likely, the government schools have had an effect. They have been working to disparage the idea of Christian explorers and settlers. We are told that the great Age of Exploration was that of gold and greed. But that is mostly false. This quote from Christopher Columbus paints a different picture than what we were fed in seventh grade. Columbus writes:

> I am a most unworthy sinner, but I have cried out to the Lord for grace and mercy and they have covered me completely. I have found the sweetest consolation since I made it my whole purpose to enjoy His marvelous presence. No one should fear to undertake any task in the name of our Savior, if it is just and if the intention is purely for His holy service.[3]

Columbus wasn't perfect, but he had a more honorable goal than monetary gain alone. The Age of Exploration and later colonialism was a mixed bag. Vishal Mangalwadi, the author of *The Book That Made Your World,* says about his country, India, "During the nineteenth century, the British evangelicals succeeded in turning the evil of colonialism into a blessing for my country."[4] Mangalwadi discusses the abuses that accompanied much of colonialism, but he also describes how this was redeemed by Christians. It is true that some elements of historic colonialism have been displeasing to God; however, the general idea of moving out and taking ground can be a faithful move—one of taking dominion for King Jesus—as long as God's ethics are not violated in the process.[5]

Modern times have produced another inhibitor of settlements: our own opinion of them. Today we tend to interpret any deliberate Christian settlement, especially rural settlements, as withdrawing from the world. The problem here, however, is that withdrawal is a complex subject. You must consider the strategic environment, mission, and opportunity to be salty. You must consider the opportunity to improve your generational position if possible and the benefits of avoiding idolatrous culture. It's a differential equation with at least eight variables. You can make arguments from the Bible in both directions. And so, we have Puritans and we have Pilgrims. I think both approaches are important if we want a full-orbed strategy.

So, what stopped the concept of the deliberate settlement? It may be difficult to pin it down to one thing. But it is worth asking ourselves, "Why don't *we* do that anymore?"

The Theology of the Christian Settlements

One cannot claim that the Christian settlement died because it was unbiblical. On the contrary, it is approved by the Bible, and its theology is rooted in the dominion mandate:

> And God blessed them, and God said unto them, Be fruit-
> ful, and multiply, and replenish the earth, and subdue it:
> and have dominion over the fish of the sea, and over the
> fowl of the air, and over every living thing that moveth
> upon the earth. (Genesis 1:28)

This dominion mandate has not gone away because it is part of the creation ordinance, "ordinances that define human ethics for all history," according to John Frame.[6]

The story of the Promised Land, the Land of Canaan, and its conquest directly uphold the concept of Christian settlements. Many today think that the Promised Land of Canaan symbolizes heaven. But, as Spurgeon pointed out, after crossing the Jordan, the Israelites did not really enter into a place of rest.[7] There were still enemies to conquer. Heaven is not that way. Heaven is a place of "done." No more tears, no more death, no enemies. It is better to understand the Promised Land as a type symbolizing the world. The promise to Abraham was that he was to be an heir of Canaan *and the world* (Gen. 12:3; 17:8; Rom. 4:13), not of heaven. And this finds fulfillment in Christ. Since Jesus is the true seed of Abraham (Gal. 3:16), He has inherited the Abrahamic promise. The world, the cosmos, *all of physical creation*, have become His (Heb. 1:2-3). We are, in a sense, co-possessors since we are in union with Him (John 15:4; Rom. 6:4-5; 8:38-39) and reigning with Him (Eph. 2:6) and ambassadors for Him (2 Cor. 5:20). The example of Joshua is helpful. When he took the Promised Land, Joshua was doing so as a type of Christ (Heb. 4:8). Likewise, we, as the army of Jesus, are to take the world (Matt. 28:18-20).

The conquest of Canaan is also very relevant to the confessional county in the sense of moving into territory that is legally Christ's but has not yet been "possessed" (Josh. 13:1). There is some *now-and-not-yet* going on here. The ultimate fulfillment rests in the new heavens and the new earth, but in the meantime, there is a lot of "possessing" that needs to happen.

Biblical support for Christian colonialism—for deliberate settlements—also comes from Paul's doctrine that if you can improve your position, go for it. "Art thou called being a servant? care not for it: but if thou mayest be made free, use it rather" (1 Cor. 7:21). Paul says, be content where you are, but realize God allows you to improve your position if possible. In the past, relocation was specifically called out as a right. The Massachusetts Body of Liberties in 1641, Article 17 said this:

> Every man of or within this Jurisdiction shall have free libertie, notwithstanding any Civill power to remove both himselfe, and his family at their pleasure out of the same, provided there be no legall impediment to the contrarie.[8]

Most likely, the people of Massachusetts had to codify the right to move out of the colony because, back then, they thought more in covenantal terms. They might have felt obligated to stay. Today, most Americans would not hesitate to pack up and move if they wanted to. But in a sense it is a right. This may become evident if the right is taken away to move when your family doesn't have all the vaccinations the government thinks you should have.

Moving, colonizing, or immigrating—call it what you like—is an exercise of freedom granted from Jesus Christ.

We Are Better Equipped Today

"If only we could get back to the time of the Pilgrims!" That's what we often say. There was a lot of good about that era. God was very gracious, and the Pilgrims were very faithful. But have we considered that their theology was actually not as good as we have been given today? Much has improved *after* the Pilgrims.

For example, we have a much better understanding of the Kingdom since Gerhard Vos came along about one hundred years ago.[9] Authors such as John Frame, Joe Morecraft, and Phil Kayser have given us a more biblically robust and practical approach to ethics than the early American pastors.

Abraham Kuyper helped us understand that society must be comprehensive (the many), and it must be all under the headship of Jesus (the One). Christendom lived this idea organically, but they probably could not defend it in a theological sense the way Kuyper could.

Also, Rushdoony helped us dust off the law like Hilkiah and "gave us the sense" in a fuller way. This had two great benefits. First, it showed us how far off we were from God's standard. Once you find the truth, it is refreshing even if convicting. With the truth, you can repent. And with repentance, you can find forgiveness and healing for the land if you are covenanted with Him. Second, it gave us a righteous way to live. The law graciously guides us into wisdom in living. "The statutes of the LORD are right, rejoicing the heart: the commandment of the LORD is pure, enlightening the eyes" (Ps. 19:8).

In Chicago in 1977, there was something of an old-fashioned church council that met. It was the "Council on Biblical Inerrancy." Higher textual criticism, the idea that not all the Bible is accurate and inspired, had been swirling around since the mid-1800s, serenading young seminary students into thinking they could outsmart the Bible. Do you know what these men did in Chicago? Working by God's grace, they put their feet on the neck of Satan and told the world we were done looking for errors in the Bible. The errors do not exist. These men killed the monster that killed many of our seminaries. They killed the monster that killed the spiritual health of beautiful settlements like Dunedin, New Zealand. I get goosebumps thinking about the spiritual forces that were torn down in Chicago when I was six years old.

But there's more, a lot more. We have many organizations today that are helping us apply the Bible to all areas of life. Generations, the Ezra Institute, Biblical Blueprints, the Chalcedon Foundation, the Center for Cultural Renewal, American Vision, and many more are teaching us how to build our lives on God's truth rather than man's. Answers in Genesis and Creation Ministries International with their scholars Ken Ham, Jason Lisle, and Jonathan Sarfati have our children rightly thinking that anything other than a six-day creation is ridiculous.

Greg Bahnsen did a fine job convincing skeptics (I was one) that the law still applies today. He and his teacher Cornelius Van Til gave us a bullet-proof way of defending the faith in the public square. Even A. A. Hodge didn't have it this good. And there are some recent improvements from people like Matt Trewhella. Trewhella revived the biblical doctrine of interposition and nullification. It seems like that came just in time. This doctrine is essential for our long-term freedom in a world system set against Christ.

We are much better equipped today in many ways, but

especially theologically, than the original colonizers of America.

Colonialism and Social Confessionalism

Colonialism (of the type presented in this book) and social confessionalism go hand in hand. There is a synergy between them. The reason is quite simple. We are societal creatures, made in the image of God. In the Trinity, there is society: structure, purpose, and companionship. When we move, we are unhitching from our local society and are more dependent upon our covenantal relationship with God. God specifically mentions that He is with us during transitions. He is the one who told Abraham to travel to an unseen land (Gen. 12:1) and the One who appeared to him along the way (Gen. 12:7).

When Moses is not sure he is up for the task at hand, what does God say? He says, "Certainly I will be with thee" (Ex. 3:12). He is the God who *brought* the Israelites out of Egypt (Ex. 20:1-2). We see the same with Joshua. Remember those words of comfort to Joshua? "Be not afraid, neither be thou dismayed: for the LORD thy God is with thee *whithersoever thou goest*" (Josh. 1:9, emphasis added). As the apostles start the Great Commission, the great *sending*, Jesus ends with the words, "Lo, I am with you" (Matt. 28:20). God is with His people in these times of transition, and once they get settled, they often covenant with God in short order.

We see this in the nature too. Mankind is not comfortable outside of society. In my travels in the military, especially when we went to remote locations, there was an urge to form social bonds. Diego Garcia was an example for me.

Diego Garcia is a tiny island in the Indian Ocean with an airport, a small naval port, and some minor infrastructure. As far as I know, it has no permanent residents. When we deployed there as a bomber squadron, we formed our own group of junior officers in no time. We had all kinds of groups. The more remote, the more the urge to bond together.

This went for my family as well. Whenever we moved to a new location, we were eager and excited to find a new church and new friends. We wanted to connect right away.

Moving into uncharted territory makes you very dependent upon God, and it makes you want to form new social bonds. The Mayflower Compact, our nation's first social confession, came about because of the precarious circumstance of literally drifting into an area not covered by the settlers' official English patent.[10] They did not want to step off that boat without some sort of covenant with God and with each other. This was the standard pattern of the early American settlements. Colonialism and social confessionalism fit together nicely.

No Place to Go

Going back to our question of why we don't practice deliberate Christian settlements today, I believe the primary reason is that we think there is no place left to go. That has probably been in the back of your mind. All the world has been claimed. There is no New World, only Old. But is this true? Look out the window on your next cross-country flight. Most of the flight, you will strain to see any signs of civilization. According to the US Census Bureau,

97 percent of the country's landmass is rural, but only 19.3 percent of the population lives there.[11]

I live in a county that has become a Mennonite settlement. Recently, we went to a community dinner hosted by the Mennonite congregation. They rented a renovated old lumber warehouse in the small downtown area and decorated it by stringing lights around the enormous rough cedar pillars. The evening started with prayer and singing, and they served *delicious* white chili. They invited many families in the community, and they won their hearts. I kept thinking to myself, "Why have Reformed families given up the idea of deliberate settlements?" After all, the Reformed faith is the faith that gave us the concept, doctrine, and practice of a Christian colony.

The Mennonite settlement started with three families and grew to over twenty families in about five years. They came from all over the US, some from Canada. They started completely over, and they are prospering today. Most of them are now leading businessmen in the county. Since the colony was so successful, they are no longer actively trying to bring more people into the settlement. Their national "colonization board" is focused on other areas. Their stated mission is, "Colonizing Rural America."

I am not saying we should become Mennonites. My point is that there are options today. You can, for example, have multiple families buy a large chunk of land and build your own town from scratch. It is just as easy today and just as legally possible as it was 150 years ago.[12]

But perhaps a more feasible approach is to move to a low-population rural county. There are plenty of those available. Land and home prices are low, as are the taxes. With 97 percent of our country being rural, you might say it is not really settled yet. Take Kansas, for example. Out of the 105 counties in Kansas, 67 of them have less than 10,000 people.[13] The idea that there is no place to go is simply not true.

I understand that moving to a rural county does not place you in another country, but it can greatly improve your standing. As we saw in chapters six and seven, God sees sub-societies as distinct. The ability to remove curses and secure blessings comes from biblical commands, biblical examples, and historical examples. Counties in the US have more sovereignty than most people realize. We got a glimpse of this during COVID when some counties refused to follow state orders. There were a lot of counties that did not fall in line, but most did not make the news because local sheriffs kept to themselves. They quietly told their deputies not to go looking for violators on Sunday mornings.[14]

Risks

It is risky, though, especially when you talk about packing up and moving to a rural county and planting a church. No matter how "solid" the families might be, they will still be made up of sinners. There will be competing ideas of what to do. How do you know if you will make new friends? There are financial risks and risks of exasperating your family. We should remember, however, that these risks also existed for the early colonizers.

Take Peter Noyes in 1638, for example. He had worked hard to build a modest but respectable living and reputation in Weyhill, Hampshire (England). But Noyes had decided. Even though winter wheat had just begun to sprout on his land, it was time to leave. After one expedition to the New World, he returned for his family and possessions. Not long after arriving with his family, Noyes found himself the unlikely leader of the new settlement of Sudbury, Massachusetts.

The settlers and their families all came with their own ideas, and Noyes was at the friction point. Sumner Chilton Powell, the author of *Puritan Village*, shows that early American settlements were often plagued with discord. He writes, "Enough disagreements arose in Noye's new community to demand over 132 town meetings and the formation of about 650 orders during Noye's lifetime in Sudbury, 1638-1657."[15] That's a lot of disagreement. When starting from scratch, people's creative ideas burst forth—and so do their opinions.

But I think we should also consider the risk of *not doing anything*. What if no Christians ever started something new again? I think we would lose a valuable skillset. There is also the risk of losing an opportunity in time. It may become harder in the future to move with increased financial hardship or travel lockdowns.

The biggest risk, however, is one close to home. When I consider all the doctrines of the Reformed faith we hold in our hands, things such as covenantal theology, a high view of Christ's reign and His law, a solid ethical framework, a positive eschatology, a durable apologetic, a theology of resistance, and a theology of beauty—all things given to us over the centuries and revived in the last fifty years, I get concerned. I am concerned we are not putting these "talents" to use. God is not pleased with that. The generational risk is significant if we keep teaching our children these doctrines with little to no opportunity to put them into practice comprehensively. Even David's faith would have fainted under those conditions. Ponder for a moment what he said:

> I had fainted, unless I had believed to see the goodness of the LORD in the land of the living. (Psalm 27:13)

I'm with David, honestly. My faith would be helped if I could see some tangible cultural progress in my lifetime. If that doesn't happen, my prayer is that I can at least get into a *structure* where my children can build in their lifetime. The deliberate Christian settlement of the past provided a way for people to start fresh and build. It has been dead since the War Between the States, but I believe God is giving us the opportunity and the reasons to revive it.

UTOPIA?

Except the LORD build the house, they labour in vain that build it.

PSALM 127:1

In 1834, the Frenchman Etienne Cabet was sentenced to five years' exile in England. His crime? He had written bitter critiques against the French government because they had not (to his satisfaction) remedied the "evil" of economic disparity. He was determined to be too liberal, even for France at the time. While in exile, he read Thomas More's book *Utopia* and was so convinced of the vision that he thought there should be a French version.

Upon returning to France, he published his new book, *Voyage to Icaria,* and attracted enough supporters to start a movement called "Icarianism." Cabet promoted the idea of Icarian colonies, and many French families committed to the adventure. The new Icarians determined the United States was the best place for communist settlements, and they set out to immigrate.

One place they chose is not far from my house. Today, the area has a beautiful lake, surrounded by gentle hills and fertile ground. It is easy to see why they chose it; I only wonder how they found it. The settlement started in 1852, and by the time of the War Between the States, it was doing very well economically by selling food and raising livestock. Tellingly, there were no religious services in this settlement. On Sundays, they would go hunting or just relax.

Of course, it did not last. Today, the area is a living history museum. The settlement survived forty-six years before disbanding in 1879. There were a couple of spinoffs (splits, really) that lived on until 1898. The average lifespan of the other six Icarian settlements across the US was seven years.

People who are considering deliberate, rural Christian settlements today are sometimes cautioned against trying to create Utopia. More than once have I been told, "There is no heaven on earth." Bonhoeffer shows this type of suspicion when he writes, "God hates visionary dreaming…the man who fashions a visionary ideal of community demands that it will be realized by God, by others, and by himself."[1] There seems to a categorical criticism of Christians who pursue a better life through settlements. Bonhoeffer is right to criticize a man-made image of a perfect community; however, I believe we should still make room for a faithful expectation of earthly, material, and societal blessings this side of heaven.

Another example of suspicion comes from *Baker's Evangelical Dictionary on Theology*, a well-respected resource. It has a section on "Utopianism." Sadly, the entire section on utopianism says nothing about what Utopia actually is. The authors write about Christian communities that thought they could achieve holiness through a greater manifestation of the Holy Spirit. They characterize utopianism as the thought that:

> ...the Holy Spirit can so bring the life of the heavenly community in to this age that...something more approaching the society of the eternal state can be realized than the church has hitherto exhibited. These are eschatological communities.[2]

If that is utopianism, sign me up. But it is not utopianism. That is simply believing what the Bible says will happen (Isa. 2:2; 11:9-10; 27:13; 56:7; Mic. 4:1-4; Acts 2:17; Heb. 1:2). The authors continue to paint various Christian communities and doctrines with their broad, misplaced brush. According to this dictionary of theology, even the Puritans were utopian with their "intense concern for sanctification."[3] I only bring this in as an example of sloppy thinking regarding utopianism.

But there are legitimate concerns. I understand why many within our circles are concerned with the concept of a Christian settlement. Historically, people have "gone off the reservation" doctrinally when they went off to start their own communities. Some of the recent idyllic communities have not gone well. However, in my research, I discovered most of these communities separated not only from their current society but also from their church. Many went off with no sending church, presbytery, or denomination. That's foolish. Just to be clear: the confessional county approach in this book does not seek to break off and be an independent church. In fact, it seeks to stay more connected to the church than most of the early American Pilgrim settlements.

Indeed, today there are some Christians who would seek to move to a new settlement for the wrong reasons. Some may have unrealistic expectations. But the confessional county is not utopian because we are looking to God's Word, along with His Spirit, as our guides. We need to remember that counterfeits are just that. We must discern between the true and the counterfeit; otherwise, both will be thrown out.

Utopian Philosophy

So if Utopia is not a bunch of "extreme," dreamy Christians, what is it? Utopia is a product of humanist thinkers and is shared by such people as Jean-Jacques Rousseau. This was the man, remember, who, while claiming to be an authority on family matters, left his five children on the steps of a hospital where they probably died. Karl Marx was also a utopian. He capitalized on More's ideas and created something we refer to today as *Marxist utopia* or *Marxist eschatology*.[4] I think John Frame nails it when he says this is nothing more than a perversion of the new heavens and the new earth of Revelation 21:1. Marx thought that people would eventually be "cured" of their profit motive. When this happens, the state will wither away. But as Frame points out, Marx's eschatology has not played out very well.

Going back to More, his central theme was unity. Unity, and the so-called peace joined to it, comes by way of the state, according to him. The state helps us cast aside the evil of social distinctions. It is not surprising that Lenin drew some of his ideas enthusiastically from More. Gordon Clark writes, "Machiavelli has acquired an unpleasant reputation, but nothing could be more revoltingly totalitarian than More's *Utopia*."[5]

Joe Boot, in his book *The Mission of God*, shows how Utopia provided a skeleton on which to hang all sorts of godless notions. A beautiful, peaceful society on earth may be the facade of utopianism, but it is miles apart from the goodness we seek in the deliberate Christian settlement. The first difference between the Christian settlement and its utopian counterfeit is who is in charge. The Bible says that it is the Lord that created all things and holds all things together (Heb. 1:2-3). Boot contrasts this with the utopian view, "Man takes the place of the mythical, nonexistent God of the Bible."[6] The utopian state assumes to itself all the attributes it sought to remove from God. Now it predestines, provides for, and ultimately saves man. Utopia starts with the rejection of God and then seeks to remake a god from man.[7] Both Christian settlements and Utopia have kingdoms, *but they have different kings.*

Creation is also seen differently. For the Christian, we see creation as declaring the glory of God and His handiwork. We are to enjoy it and take dominion over it. We see stability in seedtime and harvest; we see promises in rainbows. The utopian, however, sees man residing in a chaotic universe with no omnipotent ruler to keep things straight. In this world of chaos, freedom only makes things more chaotic. The utopian sees freedom as a threat to society. A certain amount of freedom is "necessary," says the utopian, but the chaos created by it needs to be smoothed out with collectivism.

At first glance, there seems to be a similarity between Christian settlements, particularly agrarian or semi-agrarian ones, and utopianism in that they are both connected to the land. However, the reason for this connection and the type of this connection are quite different. For the Christian, he sees land as a reward from God. God owns the land and temporarily gives it to His people for their sustenance, protection, and enjoyment. Generationally-held land is a particular blessing. "Trust in the LORD, and do good; so shalt thou dwell in the land, and verily thou shalt be fed" (Ps. 37:3).

Utopianism is different. Like the false religions of Buddhism and Hinduism, it seeks to achieve oneness with the land. Hegel brought this Eastern teaching to the West and did us no favor in doing so.[8] Marx expressed the same idea when he said man was alienated from nature but could be reunited through deliberate work. Nature is creator to the utopian. But we know that idea is sinful. It is a clear example of confusing the Creator-creature distinction (Rom. 1:25).

There is more to utopianism. Today it extends its influence to climate control, and it sees science not as discovering reality but defining and even creating it. Technology is seen not so much as helping man but extending and developing him into a more perfect and powerful condition. The main point in our short discussion is to distinguish between the blessings of beautiful Christian civilization and the perversion of it.

———————

I imagine you have heard the anecdote of how to become proficient at identifying counterfeit dollar bills. You become proficient by getting to know the real bills extremely well. If you look at a hundred real bills, the counterfeit will stand out. If we focus on the Bible's view of a blessed society, we will be able to discard the counterfeit of Utopia without too much effort.

The Lord's Prayer is the real dollar bill. And when we pray that God's will be done on earth as it is in heaven, we are dealing with authentic currency. We are praying for a construct of holiness such that our laws, culture, and even the intentions of our hearts are pleasing to God. Our thoughts are captive to Christ when heaven's ethics come down.

I do not think it is possible to pray the Lord's Prayer in faith without the expectation that God will answer soon. He would not have included the phrase "give us this day our daily bread" if God's provision and His Kingdom ethics are reserved for the by-and-by future. We simply cannot be afraid of having a civilization that worships the Lord in the beauty of holiness[9] *in our lifetimes*. In other words, there is no way to overdo this if we are doing it God's way and in His power. But we need to steer well clear of utopian ideas.

14

THE CONFESSIONAL COUNTY, PRACTICALLY

The military has an extensive planning process called the JOPP, which stands for Joint Operation Planning Process. It is a seven-step process that, in the end, provides courses of action (COAs) for a military commander to approve. Most of the plans of the military are never implemented (praise God). They sit on the shelf, ready to be dusted off if needed. Since they are built by assuming conditions, they are never perfectly suited for any condition. The old adage is: no plan survives first contact with the enemy. Still, the military has never stopped planning because it gives us a starting point, a plan to deviate from. It is in this spirit that I write this chapter.

Location

A military commander should never ask his staff, "Where should we attack?" Asking that question moves the decision space in the wrong direction—toward opinions and desires. Instead, a commander should ask, "What are the conditions we need for success?" Once that is determined, *then* you can roll out the maps. So let's walk through some of the conditions.

First of all, find a state that has good homeschooling laws. Homeschooling freedom advanced significantly from the late 1990s to about 2010. The last state to go "green" on the Homeschool Legal Defense Association (HSLDA) status map was Iowa in 2013. The momentum has stalled, and with so many government-educated children doing online classes after COVID, it will be challenging to get any more deregulation. We may even see some freedom rollback.

Homeschool laws are important for reasons beyond homeschooling. When I first moved into our small town, the police pulled up into my driveway, wanting to do a "wellness check" of people in the house. Someone allegedly called in my address as one that needed to be investigated "to make sure everyone was safe." Of course, I did not let them in without a warrant. I could stand in confidence against the police because I knew they had nothing against me. I had not registered or reported my homeschooled children, but I knew there were no requirements in my state. Had I been in another state and not registered or reported for homeschooling (I probably would do neither because of my personal convictions), there would have been recourse for the police or CPS or the local school board to push this further, especially with my pushback to the police. So homeschool laws are of great consequence.

At the state level, I recommend you pursue a state with Home Rule but not Dillon Rule. Many people, including state politicians, do not know that these are written into their state constitutions or law. A Home Rule state is one in which towns and counties can write any law they want as long as it does not contradict state and federal constitutional law.[1] A Dillon Rule state is one in which towns and counties can write their own laws, but only in the categories granted by the state. Many states have a combination of the two. The thing to remember is the states that have the most local freedom have Home Rule but not Dillon Rule.[2]

Lastly, I recommend a state that has high land freedom. By "land freedom," I mean low taxes, little-to-no building codes, and not many zoning restrictions. Having no building codes (or at least no enforcement of building codes) allows you to build a house and live in it while you finish it. This enables families to stay out of debt and still build a multi-generational house big enough to house large families. They can trim out the house as they go, maybe even finish out bedrooms only when needed.

Having low zoning restrictions allows you to split off as little or as much land as you desire for your children. It surprised me to find that some places, even in the rural Midwest, do not want you to subdivide your land into parcels of less than twenty acres. So do your research. But the main reason you want high land freedom is that God owns the land and lends it to us. The government does not own the land. When they act like they do, they are trampling on the crown rights of King Jesus.[3]

I recommend you look for a rural county with fewer than 10,000 people as a going-in rule. Those counties are less likely to have an entrenched culture, and they do not have as many established rules. When you get above 10,000 or 15,000, you will move into more of the "reform" realm than "build," and the whole reason you moved to this new county was to build. You will start to see economic development committees and entrenched, programmatic "initiatives" in larger counties.

It will be best if the location is within daily driving distance of the state capitol. State laws are important, and you want to influence them *proactively*. Also, the long-term plan will be to have someone from your settlement in the state legislature. You want your settlement to be close enough to the capital so homeschooling fathers—who also become state legislators—do not have to move away from their family or relocate for six to ten months out of the year (a typical legislative session).[4]

We have talked a lot about *creating* culture. You want to *create* culture, and you want to exercise the biblical doctrine of confessionalism. The confessional county is based on the idea that covenanting with Christ allows progress; it is not the result of progress. Indeed, small rural counties will still have a culture. However, if the culture is not strong and not immediately dangerous, you can essentially ignore it as you build another one alongside it that will eventually overtake it. The "offset" strategy we discussed, where you have the freedom to leapfrog competing forces by not directly fighting them, could be executed in rural counties in my estimation.

I have been encouraging a rural approach, but I also believe it is important *to have a town*. It would be best if a number of congregants live in the town. Remember, you are building civilization, not just community. If everyone lives on rural homesteads in different areas, you can have community but not civilization. One possible hybrid (one I personally favor) is the European village model with small acreages and a village or town in the middle. The south of England is a wonderful example. But remember, God is not against the city; He is just against the idolatry in the modern cities (and modern rural towns). The confessional county should not be afraid to have their towns grow into cities as long as you can maintain accountability and avoid pluralism.

There is a sample location criteria list in Appendix B, but of course you can make your own. In the end, you are looking for a place where you can build local Christendom, a place where the social institutions and all of society are committed to Christ and His law.

Initial Tactical Maneuvers

Once you determine a location, people can move right away as long as there is a way to worship. I know a church where six families left the city within roughly the same timeframe. They were "ready to roll" on location right away because they came with their pastor. They were living in temporary quarters, but they were all living in close proximity. It was great they could move together, but usually families cannot move all at the same time. There may be some people who have to ease out of their current location. Some may commute for a while. One pastor who successfully planted a rural church encouraged people who had to commute to have a plan to move as soon as feasible. He discouraged the commuter model, and he discouraged people from having one foot in the city and the other in the rural county. Most of his congregants listened to his counsel and eventually moved to the settlement.

Communicate expectations early. Doctrine, liturgy, music style, schedule, church program orientation, tithing, voting, children's educational approach, and many more things should be discussed beforehand. Using a denominational book of church order and constitution is a great approach. The more you can communicate beforehand, the better. I recommend the church elders lay out some initial documents and then take questions and input from potential settlers.

I would recommend having a good number of families from the outset. You want a strong initial push so that you can start worship right away, and others will have confidence that this is going to work. However, unity is more important than quantity. While you are looking for multiple families, you mostly want people committed to the same vision. Ask people what their desires and expectations are before they move and make sure it is a good fit both ways. You want at least two elders that are very similar in vision even if they have different skill sets.

When there is an opportunity to start something new, people will often come with their own preferences. That is fine. We need to remember this is Christ's church, not ours, and all parts of the body are important. We must remember to distinguish between the requirements of Scripture and the desires of people. Phil Kayser wrote a very helpful booklet titled *Belief, Liberty, and Mutual Respect*.[5] This booklet shows the circles of belief, going from the inner Christian core beliefs required of every Christian to the outer ring, which is personal preferences and liberties. Kayser writes, "Remember that good people will always have some differences until heaven." I also highly recommended everyone read Ken Sande's book, *The Peacemaker*, before venturing out. Sande gives a very practical approach to resolving conflict, which undoubtedly will be needed at some point.

Confessional Approach

Basic needs will need to be taken care of, but you want to establish a spiritual beachhead as we saw with Joshua's and Ezra's initial moves. Worship, prayer, and evangelism should start right away. Spiritual warfare should happen early and often. Satan won't like your approach. Since the idea of the confessional county is to tap into Christ's power at the outset, a covenant should be made with the representative heads of the church, heads of families and any willing Christian local magistrate as soon as possible. This will not be the all-of-society we have seen in the biblical examples, but you can call out to God for at least temporary suspension of curses.

Phase I is planned to be ten years in length. You should focus on growing the church in unity, purity, and also in numbers. Establish businesses and reach out to the community. Start to create ways to establish a culture, such as weekly lessons on American history in the community center, Christmas musicals using the historic "Lessons and Carols" program, or homeschool co-ops. Begin to select and groom men for local civil offices and perhaps the state legislature. If possible, have at least one capable Christian lawyer in the group able to defend your people.

If God prospers this endeavor, you will have others moving in. If they see that you have taken the risk and it has paid off, and if there are homes and land available for purchase (and a solid economy), others will likely move. In the introduction, I mentioned that many homeschooling families are ready and willing to move if they believe there is a good opportunity for their families.

A crucial part of this phase is to establish the respect and trust of the community. This is why most of the people need to live and work in the county. In my experience, the fastest way to establish respect is to provide quality service at good prices to the local community.

At the culmination of Phase I, you should be ready for your county to perform social confessionalism. You will have won the respect of the locals. You will have spent a decade teaching and preaching the doctrines of grace and covenant theology. You will have been evangelizing, and you will have been creating a culture of beauty and righteousness. You will have been praying fervently for a decade, casting demons out of the land. Timing is ultimately up to God, but if He is gracious, there will be cultural progress. You will have been trying to root out pluralism. Perhaps by this point, there are only Bible-believing churches in the county. If not, keep praying, preaching, and teaching.

Like we mentioned, Phase I is planned for ten years. It may take longer. But if you choose a good county and if you follow the biblical and historical practices, I see no reason why this should take hundreds of years. That would seem to be out of line with the Bible's commands *for societies* to choose "this day" whom you will serve.

The social confessions of the Bible we have surveyed in this book provide the outline of activity. A church leader should bring the Word, and there should be representative heads from the churches, the civil magistrate, and the families in the community. Representatives should confess the sins of the land and covenant with Christ as a society. The covenant should be read and signed. In a sense, you are separating yourselves from the sins of the nation by committing the county to Christ. Of course, there is no script for this, but if you need an example of a social confession, one is provided in

Appendix C. The Scottish Confessions are of course another great resource.

The confession can be official, following the example of county resolutions that formed sanctuary counties and confessional counties. Or it can be unofficial, as the confession in Nehemiah chapters nine and ten.

Phase II is where you can go forward in confidence that you have a confessional county. You can start to roll back unbiblical practices such as property taxes, government housing, and government schools. I recommend Joel McDurmon's book, *Restoring America One County at a Time*, for a detailed survey of what you can do at the county level and how to achieve it.

The strategy we laid out was to seize the initiative, get into societal blessings and realize the Kingdom in a tangible way. Local Christendom is the fighting package, and the gospel makes it possible from beginning to end. But remember this is not primarily about you and your children; it is about glorifying God and making nations jealous. Prayerfully, the next county over will say, "Surely this great nation (*or county in our case*) is a wise and under-standing people" (Deut. 4:6). Righteous judgment and laws are attractive even to unbelievers. This is when you dispatch preachers and teachers to the next county to show them a better way. This must be done with humility, recognizing and testifying to the goodness of God. Then they become a "City." And on it goes, Lord willing.

The confessional county will not be heaven on earth, but keep praying for God's ethics and grace to invade this new settlement. Do not be ashamed to call it a colony of heaven even though it is not perfect. Remember Jesus Christ our mediator has paid for the sins of the world and is now the reigning King.

Most importantly, remember this is not a novelty or a new invention. Your county will have simply returned to the normal, historical path of Reformed settlements. You may not be able to establish biblical law in short order, but you can get as close as possible and call out to God for grace. Hezekiah could not keep the Passover exactly as commanded, but He asked God for mercy, and God granted it (2 Chr. 30:2, 18-20).

15

CONCLUSION

C. S. Lewis, writing in *The Weight of Glory*, contemplates whether things temporal or eternal are greater. He concludes, of course, things eternal are greater, for "God's claim is infinite and inexorable,"[1] and there is no way to avoid it. In other words, the temporal is limited: you can leave one house and go to another or you can leave one political party and go to another, but you cannot leave God. And yet the Apostle Paul seems interested in instructing us to get on with our temporal lives and our temporal jobs. He wants us to do normal things. It would seem this exhortation is out of place with the grand writing we read (for example) in the first chapter of Ephesians. Why would the apostle write about heavenly things such as us being chosen "in Him" before the beginning of the world (Eph. 1:4), and once our hearts are so pointed upward, say something like "be ye kind one to another" (Eph. 4:32)?

The answer, C. S. Lewis writes, is this:

> All our merely natural activities will be accepted, if they
> are offered to God, even the humblest, and of all of them,
> even the noblest, will be sinful if they are not.[2]

Lewis says natural activities are accepted, no matter how plain or how elegant, if they are offered to God. The offering to God is the decisive element, and with this offering, things eternal and temporal share a common blessing of God. This concept of offering leads us to Christ, and so we find that what Lewis is really doing is retelling the theology of Ephesians 1:10:

> That in the dispensation of the fulness of times he might
> gather together in one all things in Christ, both which are
> in heaven, and which are on earth; even in him.

And this is where we began this book, reflecting on the current reign of Christ and the earthy implications of it. The kingdoms of this world have become the kingdoms of our Lord and of His Christ. Sadly, what has been missing in the new kingdoms of our Lord is the official acknowledgment of His reign. Kissing the Son, confessing Him as societies and civil magistrates, stopped happening when Christendom went away a couple of centuries ago. Kuyper's concern, that modernism pushed out Calvinism as a life-system and that life-systems are important, has proven to be legitimate. For the first time in Western history, the church is not seen as an institution, and we are living in a pool of unauthorized pluralism.

The question is, what do we do? Dreher's *Benedict Option* was the first popular book to admit that we lost the culture war. Gene Edward Veith followed quickly with his book called *Post Christian* that acknowledges Dreher's conclusion but posits his own solution. Veith appreciates Dreher's analysis of our strategic situation, yet he is not comfortable with Dreher's withdrawing element. Veith points to Jesus' request in His high priestly prayer that the Father would not take us out of the world. Instead of withdrawal, Veith offers the "Luther Option." He takes the Lutheran approach that all vocations are divinely ordained and that we should work in the world as Christians. There is nothing wrong with this in and of itself, but I think it falls short of comprehensive Christianity.

I think Dreher is closer to a real solution. Dreher admits that our current *reform* approach has not worked and offers a *build* strategy, and he has a good sense of what we are up against as "soft totalitarianism" is now pressing against us.

A big portion of our conversation has been about land curses. Land curses are social curses on earth, marked out by legislative jurisdictions and their respective geography. COVID-19 has all the qualities of a land curse, and the US has all the qualities of a cursed land. We are practicing child sacrifice in abortion, legalizing and celebrating sodomy, and even approving of sex changes for children. The critical fact of land curses is not in Dreher's work, and it is largely overlooked among conservative evangelicals. But we must realize that in order to have societal progress, we have to get out from under societal curses.

God's commands and benefits—such as evangelism, promises in the Psalms, the doctrine of the remnant, and intercessory prayer by the church for the nation—are each gracious approaches and duties to perform. Evangelism, we affirmed, is our primary strategy.[3] However, if the topic is societal righteousness and blessing, we should realize that we need societal confession if we want societal forgiveness. Simply put, forgiveness requires confession by the offender, which in the case of land curses is all-of-society with special mention of the civil magistrate. This is how the land is healed.

Leviticus 26 is an example we have not mentioned yet. The first three verses show the path to obtain blessing. Those verses require a purging of idolatry, proper Sabbath-keeping, and walking in all His statutes and commandments. Since we have not met these conditions in the US, we have not acquired the blessings of verses 4-8: rain, productive land, economic strength, peace, and God's presence. Instead, we are living in the downward-sloping verses of 14-39. The curses increase and expand as the chapter goes on. Along the way, we see God pausing to ask Israel (and us) to repent (vv. 14, 23, 27). And, once again, we see the way to find God's blessings, especially for a cursed society, is social confessionalism (vv. 40-41).

Social confessionalism is even more important since Jesus Christ became the owner of all nations today. He mediates His gracious reign through His people and the societal institutions of His own ordination. Our strategic problem is that it takes God-fearing people to make a covenant and connect to Christ. And how do we do that in a nation of 328 million people spread across 3.8 million square miles? Hopefully, I have presented a biblical way here. God uses His wide-angle lens not only to see great nations, *but also small towns and, by extension, counties.* Nehemiah showed us it's okay for a smaller society under a large and mighty pagan nation to covenant with God. His approach was not normal, but neither was his situation.

. . .

Stonewall Jackson's oblique has been the symbol for our confessional county. Marching around our culture to attack from a different angle allows us to regain the First Mover Advantage and get out of responding to the God-haters. Of course, the God-haters are not going away, and that is why it is important to get to a construct with a local civil magistrate who will interpose. We need to remember that freedom is not just so we can do what we want but so that God gets what He deserves: *pure worship and a righteous society that acknowledges Him.*

Undoing pluralism and autonomous laws and getting out from under land curses seems insurmountable, especially when we consider that you cannot go forward as a society under a curse until the society confesses. So how do we do that?

There are perhaps more ways than one to accomplish social confessionalism. But the confessional county is a solid approach, I think, especially with the current resurgence of county sovereignty. It is our oblique, and that means people have to move—not everyone, but some. Flanking maneuvers are usually done by a small unit, hopefully undetected until the strike. This book's stratagems are best suited for a low population county without a strong culture.

As Piper did by moving the "enjoying" forward in the campaign to glorify God, we seek to move confessionalism and comprehensive Christianity forward and tap in to their benefits now. Piper does not want to wait to enjoy God because he needs a way to glorify Him now. Likewise, we need a way to obey God now *as a society* because the construct of blessings and curses is presented not as a future goal but a present requirement. The City on a Hill does not come at the end of history. It exists *during history* as a "way" to make nations jealous. We saw that it takes all-of-society to show God's interdependent, institutional design. Three-bladed propellers work great if all three blades are present and in working order.

The practice of settlements breathed its last breath in the US in the late 1800s. It seems the war took the steam out of it, as it did so many other good things, slavery notwithstanding. Colonization, of the Christian-settlement type, is an expression of the dominion mandate and the Great Commission, and unless somebody somewhere revives it, part of our strategy is forfeited. There is nothing physical, economic, or even legislative preventing people from buying a large quantity of rural land and building from scratch. There is also nothing wrong, biblically speaking, with trying to take over low-population rural counties for the sake of Christ.

But this is no Utopia. We desire to build based on God's plans, not man's. Like C. S. Lewis discusses in *The Weight of Glory*, there is nothing wrong with pursuing enjoyment and the good life, but there is something wrong with doing it without God.

I want to end with the Huguenots. I think the Huguenots are a more important study for us than even the Puritans because they operated as an oppressed nation within a nation. As Aaron Renn said, we are now in the "negative world" where being a committed Christian is a social disadvantage in the US. The Huguenots would identify with us and tell us a few things. They would tell us, first of all, to sing. They used to sing going down the streets, undoubtedly singing psalms of God's glory and protection.

They would also tell us to make the best wine and become the best artisans and statesmen in the land. They would recommend we move close together because they realized too late they lived too far apart. They would tell us to focus on purity of worship, and they would tell us not to create community but rather to create civilization. They would tell us to confess Christ because He is the way, the truth, and the life. There is no other way for a person to be saved, and there is no other way for a society to be righteous:

> But the king shall rejoice in God; every one that sweareth by him shall glory: but the mouth of them that speak lies shall be stopped. (Psalm 63:11)

APPENDIX A: MAXIMS AND STRATAGEMS OF LOCAL CHRISTENDOM

MAXIMS OF LOCAL CHRISTENDOM

I. Christ's mediatorial reign has changed everything.

- As demonstrated in the early gospel presentations, Jesus is the new King of the earth (Acts 2:30-36; Acts 17:7; 1 Tim 1:17; Rev. 11:15).
- There will be a total renovation of creation later, but we are living in the early stages of the new heavens and the new earth now (Isa. 2; Rom. 8:22; 1 Cor. 7:31; 15:20-25; Col. 1:10; Heb. 12:22).

II. Christianity is necessarily comprehensive, and this comprehensiveness is required today.

- There are four elements to Christian comprehensiveness: All the law (Deut. 27:26; 28:1, 15; 32:46; Josh. 11:15); all the people (Prov.

13:24; 22:6; Eph. 6:4); all the geographical area of any given place (Deut. 28:3; Josh. 11:23); and all our hearts (Deut. 30:10).

- Comprehensiveness is a present-day requirement, requiring present-day action. It is not presented as a future goal. This does not mean we will obtain perfection immediately. That comes gradually (Ex. 23:30; Luke 13:19, 21; Phil. 1:6; Heb. 12:28). But it means there is a requirement for each society to choose "this day" what path they are going to commit to covenantally (Deut. 30:11, 19-20; Josh. 24:15).

- The three social organizations that God authorized and instituted are the family (Deut. 6:6-9; Eph. 6:4), the church (Deut. 4:10; Matt. 16:18; Heb. 3:6; 1 Pet. 2:9), and the civil magistrate (Ex. 18:21; 2 Sam. 23:3; Rom. 13:4). Each of these have qualifications for officers, specific ethical and functional requirements, and codified accountability to each other. Only with all three institutions operating under the same covenantal connection to Christ and His law will Christian society operate as designed. Only in this way can the City on a Hill work. Community is not enough. We need biblical civilization, even if it's small.

- While all three institutions are required to confess Christ as Lord, the Bible places a specific emphasis on the civil magistrate (Ps. 2:10-11; Matthew 10:18; Acts 9:15; 26:28-29). This requirement was codified with the Coronation of Christ, when the kingdoms of this world became the kingdoms of our Lord (Rev. 11:15).

III. Pluralism and autonomous laws prevent societal blessings.

- The conditions for blessings do not allow pluralism in the land (Ex. 12:49; 23:24-33; Deut. 7:4-6; 13:12-18; 17:1-7; Acts 17:22-31). The kings that did not remove the high places displeased God: Asa (1 Kings 15:14), Jehoshaphat (1 Kings 22:42. Note: Jehoshaphat did remove the sodomites from the land and that pleased God), Jehoash (2 Kings 12:3), Amaziah (2 Kings 14:4). Hezekiah, however, did remove the high places and "brake the images" and thus pleased the Lord. (2 Kings 18:4-5).
- Pluralism is polytheism and therefore idolatry. Any religion other than Christianity is idolatry (Ex. 13:1-16; 20:4; Gal. 1:8). Worshipping according to the commandments of men is also idolatry (Matt. 15:9; Col. 2:23). Idolatry in the land places us under curses (Lev. 26:1, 14-39; Deut. 27:15). The Lord owns all the earth, so idolatry is not allowed anywhere (Ps. 24:1).
- The Lord is opposed to autonomous laws (Judg. 21:25; Prov. 14:12; Matt. 5:17; 15:3, 6; Mark 7:9).

IV. Land curses apply to all nations, and they apply in the new covenant.

- The land of all nations, not just Israel, is defiled when God's commandments are broken (Lev. 18:24-25).
- Land curses still apply in the new covenant (Ps. 2:8; Matt. 7:12; 10:14-15; 15:4; Acts 13:51).

V. The United States is under land curses.

- Specific land curses come from: 1. Killing the innocent (Num. 35:33-34; Ps. 106:38); 2. Sexual Immorality (Lev. 18:24-25); 3. Sabbath-breaking (Neh. 13:17-18); 4. Idolatry (Lev. 26:1, 14). Additionally, societies who do not follow "all his commandments and all his statues" receive the curses of Deuteronomy 28:17-68.
- The four specific land curses come from sins that are also crimes. Therefore the main responsibility of the land curses above lies in the civil magistrate's jurisdiction. God's law is violated whenever these sins occur, and God's law is also violated when these sins are not punished according to His law (Num. 35:33).

VI. You cannot find overall societal success when under a societal curse.

- The overall status of a society is presented as either blessed or cursed (Deut. 30:19; Ps. 9:17; 33:12). There are varying levels of blessings or curses, however.
- Only God can remove a curse He has levied (Isa. 14:27; 43:13).
- A curse must be removed before our overall mission can go forward. See the account of the first attack of Ai and Achan's sin (Josh. 7). After removing the curse, the Israelites were successful (Josh. 8). Also, the community under Haggai had to remove their land curse through social

confession before finding success in building the temple (Hag. 1).

VII. Land curses are geospatial and are tied to the society that lives there. Blessings are also geospatial and tied to the society that lives there. This provides a way for us to secure blessings.

- God differentiates between towns when levying His curses (Gen. 18:20; 19:13, 25; Isa. 17:1; Matt. 10:14-15; 11:21; Acts 13:51). The land of Goshen was protected from plagues (Ex. 8:22). This means towns or counties have the opportunity to be removed from the land curses of the greater nation.

VIII. Social confessionalism is presented in the Bible as an approved model for societies to move from curses to blessings.

- Social confessionalism is consistent with covenant theology. Only by Christ's power can we even begin to have a righteous society (Dan. 9:18; Eph. 2:5). Only by covenant is Christ's power available to us (Deut. 7:9; Ps. 103:18; John 15:5).
- God sees societies (nations, regions, towns) as corporate entities which can and should covenant with Him (Ps. 33:12).
- Social covenants where all-of-society stands to the covenant in order to secure blessings is presented as a way out of societal (land) curses. Often this was in light of their sin and need of

God's grace. Examples include Moses and the people (Ex. 19:7-8); the covenant renewed under Moses (Deut. 29:13); Joshua and the assembly (Josh. 1:16-18; 24:24-25); and kings with their people, such as Jehoiada (2 Kin. 11:17); Josiah (2 Kin. 23:3); and Asa (2 Chr. 15:9, 12).

IX. Social confessionalism can remove curses and secure blessings for lesser civil societies even if the greater civil society is not covenanted with God.

- Upon returning from exile, the lesser civil societies under Ezra and Nehemiah covenanted. They did not even ask for permission from their rulers, the Persian kings Cyrus and later Darius (Ezra 10:1-12; Neh. 10:28-29). The covenant in Nehemiah is particularly important for four reasons: (1) it is the closest to the situation of a rural county today (with its own civil jurisdiction and yet under the jurisdiction of another); and (2) It was accomplished in the midst of an area full of God-haters; (3) It shows how representative heads from the civil magistrate (Neh. 10:1), the church (Neh. 10:2-13), and the families signed the covenant (Neh. 10:28); (4) They covenanted early in their new civilization.

X. Other societal approaches, such as evangelism, protection afforded in the Psalms, the doctrine of the remnant, and intercessory prayer are beneficial but are not presented as a normative way to remove curses and secure blessings.

- Evangelism is our primary offensive weapon and duty. It is the precondition of any righteous society. However, personal confession of Christ does not remove the sins of the land (2 Chr. 7:14).

- The Psalms offer protection for God's people even in the midst of curses (Ps. 37; 91). However, they are not presented as a way to remove long-term geographical curses.

- The doctrine of the remnant may preserve society from God's wrath (Gen. 18:32; 1 Kin. 19:18; Ezra 9:8; Ezek. 22:30). But overall it is defensive in nature, preserving God's people. It is more a condition than a strategy.

- Intercessory prayer by the church can do two things. (1) It can delay/stop judgment (Num. 16:46-49); (2) It can spur on revival (Ezra 9:5-10, 12). However, intercessory prayer by the church cannot secure forgiveness for the nation or heal the land (Gen. 18:33; 19:24; Ex. 32:11-14, 34-35; Ezra 9:5-15; 10:1, 9-12; Jer. 11:14). Civil sins require civil and societal confession (2 Chr. 7:14). See chapter eight for a more complete exegesis of these three approaches.

- All these protective approaches should still be prayed for even if we do not meet the conditions perfectly (2 Chr. 30:1, 18), but they do not replace social confessionalism as the way to move from curses to blessings as a society.

STRATAGEMS OF LOCAL CHRISTENDOM

I. Build local Christendom in current history as a "way" to the "end" of worldwide gospel victory in the future.

- The blessings of Deuteronomy 28 are contingent on all of society keeping all the law. Those blessings are described as present-day requirements to secure present-day and generational blessings.
- Comprehensive, covenantal society (aka Christendom) occurs in history, showing God's glory and making nations jealous (Is. 2:2; Rev. 21:3).
- The "last days" commensurate with the mountain of the Lord are not at the end of history but began in 1400 BC and expired in AD 70. This Mountain is established to enable the growth of God's Kingdom, not to demonstrate its completion (Mic. 4:1-2; Acts 2:17; Heb. 1:2).
- The Great Commission shows us God's grand strategy of comprehensiveness ("whatsoever commanded") and confessionalism ("nations, baptizing them in the name of the Father, and of the Son, and of the Holy Ghost . . . I am with you alway") as contemporary with current gospel campaign actions, not a distant result of them.
- The City on a Hill strategy shows that a small segment can have broad effects. One town—

Magdeburg, Germany—probably saved the Reformation.

II. Colonize rural counties as a faithful expression of the dominion mandate for all ages.

- The concept of new settlements is based in the dominion mandate (Gen. 1:28). The conquest of Canaan was a type of Christians taking the whole world for Christ in fulfillment of the Abrahamic covenant (Gen. 12:3; 17:8; Josh. 1:8-9; 13:1; Rom. 4:13; Gal. 3:16). Colonization is a strategy still available to us today.
- God approves of us moving in order to better our condition (1 Cor. 7:21). Early pilgrims saw the right to move as a gift from God, and they believed that some Christians who engaged in colonizing would help all Christians everywhere.
- We are in a better place today for deliberate Christian settlements than we have ever been. Our doctrine is better, the risks are lower, and the opportunities are roughly the same as in the past. Strategic analysis concludes that timing is good for a second wave of Christian settlements today.

III. Confess Christ locally as a way to tap into the power of Christ, remove curses and secure blessings.

- Covenants can be renewed or created from scratch (Deut. 29:1).
- Covenants can be created in sub-societies

without permission from higher civil authorities (Neh. 9:38).

- Building rather than reforming allows us to establish First Mover Advantage (Josh. 10:9; 11:7). It also may allow us to become freed from the curses associated with autonomous laws (Matt. 15:3; Mark 7:9) and pluralism (Ex. 20:3; Deut. 6:4; Jer. 35:15).

- The Bible presents all-of-society, "social confessionalism," as the way to move out of curses into blessings. All the people stand to the covenant (Ex. 19:7-8; Deut. 27:15-26; 29:13; Josh. 24:24-25; 2 Kin. 11:17; 23:3; 2 Chr. 15:9, 12; Ezra 10:12; Neh. 9:38). If anything, this is more relevant and an even greater requirement after the coronation of Christ than it was in the Old Testament (Ps. 2:10-12).

- The concept of geospatial blessings and curses is still in effect today (Gen. 18:20-21; 19:13, 25; Isa. 17:1; Matt. 10:14-15, 11:21; Acts 13:51).

IV. Worship in holiness and create beautiful culture.

- Worship can stake Christocentric claims upon the geographical areas Christians inhabit (Josh. 5:5; Ezra 3:3). Spiritual warfare can be leveraged geographically. Demons are not omnipresent and can be forced out of geographical areas through spiritual warfare (Matt. 8:28; Mark 5:10; Luke 11:24; Rev. 9:14).

- Antithesis is a force-enhancer, showing the beauty of God's culture versus the ugliness of autonomous man's (Deut. 4:6; Isa. 2:2; Mic. 4:1-2; Matt. 5:14-16).

V. Leverage localism and the structure of counties.

- God's covenants are land-based (Gen. 1:29-30; 17:8; Deut. 26:1; 28:8; 2 Chr. 7:14; Ps. 37:29; Matt. 5:5; Rom. 4:13).
- Our states are sovereign entities per the constitution. We can leverage the rising decentralization that is due to federal overreach and increasingly disparate cultures in America.
- Localism enables the type of face-to-face and institutional accountability needed for a righteous society. Without localism, mankind's depravity gains influence. Localism is the primary picture of society we see in the Bible, where rulers interacted with people often (Prov. 23:1-3).
- There are typically only five elected offices at the county level in the US. Engaging the primary elections before the general election may enable us to get qualified Christians in office in a relatively short time.
- Even if we cannot get to full biblical law in the county in the short term, the Lord may grant mercy to us if we confess our desires formally even though we cannot yet officially. The county resolutions that are being made today against abortions (sanctuary counties) are good examples of this formal but unofficial method. Hezekiah could not keep the Passover exactly as

commanded, but he asked God for mercy, and God granted it (2 Chr. 30:2, 18).

VI. Execute the doctrine of the lesser magistrate to maintain long-term freedom and righteousness.

- Resistance to God-hating government will be necessary to maintain freedom, but this should be done through the lesser magistrate. The county is well-suited for this (Jer. 29:16-31; Dan. 3:12, 16-18; Rom. 13:1, 4).
- True freedom is not freedom for ourselves but for Christ's crown rights. If we allow the state to take away freedoms that Christ has granted, we live in practical denial of biblical truth (John 8:36; Gal. 5:1; Jas. 1:25). Where the Spirit of the Lord is, there is liberty (2 Cor. 3:17). Failure to resist unbiblical laws may lead to generational punishment upon a society (Jer. 36:31).

APPENDIX B: LOCATION CRITERIA

This location criteria is not set in stone. Each group of settlers would naturally set their own criteria, but these are some of the things I have developed after researching and visiting successful rural Christian counties.

STATE CRITERIA

- State has good homeschooling laws.
- State allows counties to set blue laws (laws restricting activity on the Lord's Day).
- State is one where property taxes go primarily or exclusively to the local county. This will make it easier to get rid of property taxes.
- State upholds the death penalty for capital crimes.
- State is one where the culture is supportive of freedom and has a willingness to resist, when

necessary or when convenient, federal government encroachment.

- State has Home Rule but not Dillon's Rule.[1]
- State population should not be increasing rapidly due to transplants, especially from the Northeast, California, or foreign countries.

COUNTY CRITERIA

- County should be small, ideally less than 10,000 people. This allows for us to build culture in 10-20 years rather than slowly reform it. This assumes the settlement starts from scratch. If you move to a county that has a church already established with a number of families, the county could be larger.
- County should not have urban sprawl from a neighboring city or county.
- County should not have a major college or university since these institutions are (over the long-term) a primary source of pluralism and anti-Christian philosophy. This does not necessarily mean we could not set up our own.
- Land is inexpensive (<$4,000 per acre) and readily available for purchase in small plots (5-40 acres). This allows for people to live close together. This does not mean everyone has to live in the country.
- Property taxes should be less than $2,000 a year on a $250,000 house.
- There should not be national chain retail stores

that would fight against Sabbath laws (and likely win with their army of lawyers).

- Ideally there should be no strong and sustainable culture such as well-funded and/or well-respected government schools.
- Ideally there would not be a strong entitlement culture of county welfare and housing, etc.
- Ideally there would not be God-hating families of extreme wealth that can influence people negatively.
- There should be no federal agency that employs more than a few people.
- Ideally there would be no state agency that employs more than a few people.

TOWN CRITERIA

- Town should be the county seat and have less than 3,000 people.
- Town should be within an hour and a half's travel (1:30) of the state capital. This will allow easy access and will enable our sons to be state representatives.
- Town should be no closer than one hour and no further than an hour and a half's travel (1:00-1:30) from a major metropolitan area. Being greater than an hour allows for distinct local culture and economy. Remember the city will grow over generations. Being less than an hour and a half's distance allows access to job markets (commuting is not desired but may be necessary

for short-term employment), advanced medical, travel, specialty shopping, etc.

AREA CRITERIA

- Landscape is beautiful and abundant in natural resources. Water should be readily available and clean.
- Area should have a good amount of trees for security and survival.
- Ideally soil should be fertile and have a good amount of rain for growing crops.
- Area should be one to which people are generally willing to move.
- Ideally area should have a moderate climate that includes some snow since many people like that.

APPENDIX C: SAMPLE COUNTY CONFESSION

Preamble. Modified from the Solemn League and Covenant

We the Civil Magistrates, Ministers of the Gospel, and Fathers, in the County of _____, by the providence of GOD, living under the reign of King Jesus and having in mind the advancement of His gracious and beautiful Kingdom and the happiness of ourselves and of future generations, recognizing the legal authority of the Constitution of the United States and the Constitution of the State of _____, yet seeing the failure of those signers to proclaim God's reign and His law as our ethical standard, we hereby Covenant with each other and with our Lord Jesus Christ. We proclaim God has granted us this authority in that He holds all societies accountable and offers them to choose this day whom they will follow, and that Nehemiah demonstrated the right to covenant as a subordinate civil society under the non-covenanted nation of Persia, and that without permission, with our hand lifted up to the Most High GOD, do swear,[1]

Section 1. The Nature of God and His Relation to Man, from the Magdeburg Confession [2]

Concerning the nature of God, we declare and teach against heretics ancient and modern from the certain Word of God, according to the declaration of the Apostolic, Nicene, and Athanasian Creeds, that there is one God, the Father, Son, and Holy Spirit, that is, three persons, indivisible, intelligent, and incommunicable, of the same substance, of infinite power and glory, equally from eternity.

Likewise we confess that the Son was made man, conceived of the Holy Spirit, born of the virgin Mary, so that our Lord Jesus Christ should be true God and true man, with His body and rational soul thus united with the eternal Word of the Father in one person, because by this union Christ is God and man, but by His free or voluntary humiliation and kenosis. He really suffered, was crucified, died, and was buried; He descended to the dead according to the will of the Father; on the third day He was made alive again and ascended into heaven, and sits at the right hand of the Heavenly Father, ruling with equal power with the Father for all eternity; who shall come again with majesty to do universal judgment on the entire human race. And when the resurrection of all the dead has happened, He shall repay each one according to his works; that is, to those who have repented and trusted in Him, He shall give possession of the inheritance of God in eternal life; but the rest, the impenitent and unbelieving, He shall subject together with the Devil to the penalty of damnation and eternal death.

Section 2. The Chicago Statement of Biblical Inerrancy

1. God, who is Himself Truth and speaks truth only, has inspired Holy Scripture in order thereby to reveal Himself to lost mankind through Jesus Christ as Creator and Lord, Redeemer and Judge. Holy Scripture is God's witness to Himself.

2. Holy Scripture, being God's own Word, written by men prepared and superintended by His Spirit, is of infallible divine authority in all matters upon which it touches: it is to be believed, as God's instruction, in all that it affirms; obeyed, as God's command, in all that it requires; embraced, as God's pledge, in all that it promises.

3. The Holy Spirit, Scripture's divine Author, both authenticates it to us by His inward witness and opens our minds to understand its meaning.

4. Being wholly and verbally God-given, Scripture is without error or fault in all its teaching, no less in what it states about God's acts in creation, about the events of world history, and about its own literary origins under God, than in its witness to God's saving grace in individual lives.

5. The authority of Scripture is inescapably impaired if this total divine inerrancy is in any way limited or disregarded, or made relative to a view of truth contrary to the Bible's

own; and such lapses bring serious loss to both the individual and the Church.

Section 3. Public Confession and Covenant [3]

We hereby covenant with our Father, our Lord Jesus Christ, and the Holy Spirit to stay true to the following convictions in our hearts and to work for them diligently in our families, our churches, and our community. While signing this covenant, we recognize that in God's sovereignty our current culture's civil laws are out of accord with our convictions. While we see the necessity to change numerous laws and to do that as soon as reasonably possible, we desire a peaceful transition and resolve to pray and work to that end.

We acknowledge these truths from God's Word as applicable for all people in all times and places. We ask God to receive our prayer specifically for our land and appropriate to us His gracious forgiveness. We know that in times past God overlooked ignorance but now calls all men everywhere to repent (Acts 17:30).

1. Jesus Christ is Lord of the nations, and therefore He is Lord of this county. We repent of our failure to recognize Your Son properly and openly (Matt. 28:18; Acts 10:36; 1 Cor. 15:27; Phil. 2:9-11).

2. The civil magistrate operates on delegated authority from God and is responsible to Him (Ps. 2:1-12; 72:8; 110:1-7; Matt. 28:18). We repent that we have regarded our civil officials primarily as servants of men rather than ministers of You, our Lord.

3. The moral laws given in the Ten Commandments are binding for all people of all time. They form the basis for morality and the foundation for law (Deut. 11:1; Ps.

119:44; Isa. 42:4; 2 Pet. 2:6-8). We repent of our previous enacting of unbiblical laws at the national, state, and local levels. We repent of the fact that biblical laws have been removed from our civil law code. We repent of the fact we have not set laws to uphold Your moral law.

4. Only Christian men in good standing in an evangelical church are qualified to hold public office (Ex. 18:21; Deut. 1:13; Judg. 8:22; Isa. 3:4, 12; 1 Tim. 2:11-13). We repent of electing and supporting men who are not qualified according to Your standards. We repent of electing and supporting women to civil offices.

5. The Christian faith is a public faith and makes claims upon all areas of life (Isa. 12:4; 45:22; Acts 5:28-32). We repent of laws and interpretations of laws that contravene Your command for us to proclaim Your name throughout the land. We repent of not calling men to repent and to obey the gospel.

6. Abortion is murder and therefore breaks the Sixth Commandment and is a capital crime (Ex. 20:13; 21:22-24; Lev. 18:21; Job 3:3; Ps. 139:13-16; Luke 1:15). We repent of any abortion in our country, state, and county. We repent of not punishing abortion according to Your law, and we ask that You heal our county and forgive us. We resolve that no abortion will be allowed to take place in our county. Please help us.

7. Homosexuality is listed in multiple areas of the Bible as being a capital crime (Lev. 18:22-25; Rom. 1:26-28; 1 Cor. 6:9). We repent for allowing deliberate, public, unrepentant homosexuality in our nation, state, and county. Please heal the land of our county and forgive us.

8. Adultery is a capital crime, and our failure to punish this crime has defiled the land (Ex. 20:14; Lev. 20:20; Jer. 3:9). We repent of this sin and our lack of

punishing it. Please, Lord, heal the land of our county and forgive us.

9. The Fourth Commandment requires businesses to be closed on the Christian Sabbath (the first day of the week) unless necessary for basic needs (Gen. 2:3; Ex. 16:26; 20:8-11; Neh. 13:17-19). Lord, we repent of not keeping the Sabbath holy. Please forgive us.

10. The Heidelberg Catechism Q&A 95 says, "idolatry is having or inventing something in which one trusts in place of or alongside of the only true God, who has revealed himself in the Word." Lord, we repent of the fact that our county has wrongly put false gods before You (Ex. 20:3; Rom. 1:23) and has worshiped according to the commandments of men instead of according to Your laws (Matt. 15:9; Col. 2:23). We repent of allowing idolatry in our land and pledge to remove it as quickly as possible. Please help us.

— Signed by our own hand and of our own volition —

APPENDIX D: WHAT YOU CAN DO AT THE COUNTY LEVEL

At the county level, the opportunity to connect to Christ covenantally as a society and to follow His laws comprehensively is the main benefit. As we have seen, the Bible shows this is a way to remove curses and secure blessings while at the same time being a City on a Hill for God's glory. But there are many other benefits joined to this.

Furthermore, it's not that difficult to get your people into county positions. There are really only a few elected officials in a rural county: the commissioners (usually three to five), the sheriff, the district attorney, and the auditor. In conservative counties where Republicans win by wide margins, the real election is the primary, not the general election. In Montgomery County, Iowa, a county of 10,760 people, every one of the county positions can be carried with only 362 votes in the primary election.

Official Policy

- Become "sanctuary counties" for the unborn,[1]

like Yadkin County, NC did on August 19, 2019; or for the 2nd Amendment, like over 120 counties did in Virginia in 2019 to 2020.

- Become a "constitutional county." This is a new development that has arisen post-COVID-19 as counties realized that it is more than gun rights at stake.[2]
- Property tax can be reduced or in some cases eliminated and replaced with a more biblical head tax.[3]
- Eliminate government schools in the county.
- Set county blue laws to reduce retail on the Sabbath to only necessary items.
- Eliminate unbiblical welfare programs.
- Set county ordinances to prohibit pornography and "adult" venues.

Influence from Elected County Officials

- Sheriff can protect rights of parents and provide a check on federal overreach.
- County attorney can positively influence how violations are dealt with.
- County commissioners can eliminate unbiblical funding of social programs.
- All government officials can dissuade CPS from unbiblical kidnapping.

Influence from the Church

- Gospel outreach.
- Community education on the biblical basis of freedom.

- Show beauty of the gospel through music and community services.

Influence from Families and General Culture

- Make it undesirable for homosexuals to move in and defile the land.
- Create businesses.
- Beautify county.

For more information on what you can do at the county level, get a copy of *Taking America One County at a Time* by Joel McDurmon.

NOTES

INTRODUCTION

1. Rod Dreher, *The Benedict Option: A Strategy for Christians in a Post-Christian Nation* (New York: Penguin, 2017), 12.
2. P. Andrew Sandlin, *Religion Realized* (Coulterville: Center for Cultural Leadership, 2021), Kindle Edition, Preface.
3. We also see society in terms of other institutions: sports and entertainment, media, academia, and Big Tech. These, I submit, are unauthorized institutions and should not even exist in their current institutional form, but we'll table that discussion for another time.
4. I realize that the City on a Hill is a metaphor; however, the societal element of God's redemptive plan runs through the whole Bible. Deuteronomy 4:6-7 is not metaphorical at all. It's a real, comprehensive nation showing God's glory and compelling other nations to follow Him.

1. THE OBLIQUE

1. The full quote is: "The enemy has made a stand at Chancellor's, which is about two miles from Chancellorsville. I hope, so soon as practicable, to attack. I trust that an ever kind Providence will bless us with success." It was Jackson's last memo to General Lee.
2. This is probably the only thing we should emulate from Frederick the Great. He was the patron of the Enlightenment, friend of Voltaire, and founder of the Berlin Academy that produced Kant. The Enlightenment is what set us on the dubious cultural path we find ourselves on today. Gene Edward Veith, Jr., *Post-Christian* (Crossway Books, 2020), 211.
3. Robert Lewis Dabney, *Life and Campaigns of Lieutenant General Thomas J. Stonewall Jackson* (Harrisonburg: Sprinkle Publications, 1983), 672.
4. Sigmund Neumann and Mark Von Hagen, "Engels and Marx on Revolution, War, and the Army in Society," *Makers of Modern Strategy: From Machiavelli to the Nuclear Age* (Princeton: Princeton Press, 1986), 265.

5. Paul Michael Raymond, "Tactical Considerations for a Biblical Reformation," *Faith for All of Life*, November/December 2014, accessed January 11, 2021, https://chalcedon.edu/magazine/tactical-considerations-for-a-biblical-reformation.

6. *"ex nihilo"* is Latin for "out of nothing."

2. SITUATION REPORT

1. Dreher, *The Benedict Option*, 8. Dreher was speaking of the death of Christianity in the West, not the whole world

2. PRRI Staff, "Dueling Realities: Amid Multiple Crises, Trump and Biden Supporters See Different Priorities and Futures for the Nation," October 19, 2020, accessed February 2, 2021, https://www.prri.org/research/amid-multiple-crises-trump-and-biden-supporters-see-different-realities-and-futures-for-the-nation/.

3. Isaiah 66:4 shows us that God makes a society delusional and fearful when we stop listening to God. "I also will choose their delusions, and will bring their fears upon them; because when I called, none did answer; when I spake, they did not hear: but they did evil before mine eyes, and chose that in which I delighted not" (Isa. 66:4).

4. The "School of Athens" is a popular painting by Italian Renaissance artist Raphael. It was painted between 1509 and 1511 and depicts Plato and Aristotle. Raphael was commissioned to paint it for the Vatican. Gary DeMar, *God and Government* (Powder Springs, Georgia: American Vision, 2011), 233.

5. Autonomy is a variation of the original sin. It ignores God's Word and ethic and seeks to establish our own.

6. Matthew J. Trewhella, *The Doctrine of the Lesser Magistrates: A Proper Resistance to Tyranny and a Repudiation of Unlimited Obedience to Civil Government* (North Charleston: CreateSpace Independent Publishing Platform, 2013), 21.

7. Trewhella, *Doctrine of the Lesser Magistrates*, 22. Trewhella quotes William Blackstone, *Commentaries on the Laws of England, vol. 1* (Philadelphia, PA: Childs & Peterson 1765/1860), 42.

8. Winton U. Solberg, *Redeem the Time: The Puritan Sabbath in Early America* (Harvard University Press, 1977), 193. Roger Williams was the first to introduce the idea of a religiously pluralistic society. His views were seen by most as striking and dangerous.

9. Philip B. Kurland and Ralph Lerner, eds., *The Founders' Constitution*. Vol. 1. (University of Chicago Press, 1987), 3.

10. The Bible says there can only be one law, God's law, for all people, even "strangers" (Ex. 12:49), but it also says we should respect and protect the "strangers" (Ex. 22:21). A non-Christian may not realize

it, but he would be safer in a truly Christian society than a God-hating one.

11. Aaron M. Renn, "The Lost World of American Evangelicalism," *The Masculinist #13*, September 14, 2017, accessed February 2, 2021, https://themasculinist.com/the-masculinist-13-the-lost-world-of-american-evangelicalism/.

12. Gary Scott Smith, *God and Politics: Four Views on the Reformation of Civil Government* (P & R Publishing Company, 1989), 106.

13. Gary North, *Political Polytheism: The Myth of Pluralism* (Tyler: Institute for Christian Economics, 1989), 7.

14. Smith, *God and Politics*, 115.

15. For an evaluation of our constitution from a confessionalist perspective, see *Explicitly Christian Politics*, edited by William O. Einwechter (Pittsburg, PA: The Christian Statesman Press, 2001).

16. David Scott, *Distinctive Principles of the Reformed Presbyterian Church* (Albany: Munsell, 1841), 14.

3. LAND CURSES

1. "A possible alternative translation model for these verses is: Yahweh will punish you by giving you few children and poor crops: Your cattle and sheep won't produce many young: 19 He will make you fail [or be unsuccessful] in everything you do." Robert G. Bratcher and Howard A. Hatton, *A Handbook on Deuteronomy*, UBS Handbook Series (New York: United Bible Societies, 2000), 452.

2. Bratcher and Hatton, *Handbook on Deuteronomy*, 452.

3. Note: The actual word is "pestilence," and it will continue until God kills as many people as He intends (Deut. 28:22).

4. When you look at this chart, you'll notice another curse besides the economy—you'll see war (Ezek. 14:17).

5. Of course the curses against Egypt are another example of non-Israelite nations being under curses.

6. Blessings and curses are part of the package of God's law. Joshua read "all the words of the law, the blessings and cursings, according to all that is written in the book of the law" (Josh. 8:34).

7. See Rushdoony's audio series, "The Theology of the Land."

8. The case laws are taken from Exodus 21:1-23:33. These give examples of how to apply the Decalogue in everyday life.

9. Some think that in John 8:11 Jesus nullifies the civil penalty for adultery when He tells the adulteress "Neither do I condemn thee." But Jesus' concern was to show the Pharisees were relying on the tradition of men. When Jesus called for witnesses (the lawful thing required), they shirked away, and the civil case was canceled. Of

note, Jesus tells the lame man in John 5:14, "Go and sin no more, lest a worse thing come upon thee." He seems to be upholding punishment in the midst of correcting the Pharisees. See Rousas John Rushdoony, *The Institutes of Biblical Law, vol. 1* (P & R Publishing Co., 1973), 705-706. Finally, Paul also upheld the case law with the muzzled ox verse (1 Cor. 9:9).

10. See also Psalm 106:38 and Leviticus 18:21.

11. R. J. Rushdoony, "The Theology of the Land," Rushdoony Radio, https://rushdoonyradio.org/theology-of-the-land/.

12. *Crime in the United States, 2018,* Uniform Crime Report (Criminal Justice Information Services Division), accessed February, 2021, https://ucr.fbi.gov/crime-in-the-u.s/2018/crime-in-the-u.s.-2018/topic-pages/murder. Note: These statistics do not include murders committed by abortion.

13. *Crime in the United States, 2018,* accessed February, 2021, https://ucr.fbi.gov/crime-in-the-u.s/2018/crime-in-the-u.s.-2018/topic-pages/murder.

14. "2018 Abortion Data Table," accessed February, 2021, https://abort73.com/images/2018-abortion-data-table.png. The number reported to the CDC was 619,591. Katherine Kortsmit, PhD et al., "Abortion Surveillance—United States, 2018" *Surveillance Summaries,* November 27, 2020, accessed , https://www.cdc.gov/mmwr/volumes/69/ss/ss6907a1.htm.

15. Holly Honderich, "In Trump's final days, a rush of federal executions," BBC News, Washington, January 16, 2020, accessed , https://www.bbc.com/news/world-us-canada-55236260.

16. Westminster Confession of Faith 21.8. Note: Some conservative Reformed churches today do not hold that recreation is prohibited. They have in mind some minor games and exercises as fellowship activities. But this is different from institutionalized sports on the Lord's Day, which would clearly not be an act of necessity or mercy.

17. William Bradford, *Of Plymouth Plantation, 1620-1647* (New York: Rutgers University Press, 1952), 25.

18. Joseph C. Morecraft, *Authentic Christianity: An Exposition of the Theology and the Ethics of the Westminster Larger Catechism (5 volumes)* (American Vision, 2009), Volume 4, 504-505. Dr. Morecraft provides a succinct and convincing argument for the requirement of the Sabbath today.

19. See Leviticus 26:1, 2. Blessings are granted for not having idolatry or breaking the Sabbath, but then curses are listed in verse 14 to the rest of the chapter.

20. Walter A. Elwell, *Evangelical Dictionary of Theology* (Baker Academic, 2001), 589.

21. Calvin says the Romish practice of adoration is idolatry. Calvin, *The Necessity of Reforming the Church*, accessed March, 2021, https://www.monergism.com/necessity-reforming-church-ebook, 10. Rushdoony says the same. Rushdoony, *The Institutes of Biblical Law, vol. 1*, 39.

22. See also Westminster Confession 23.3 which states that the civil magistrate should see that "all blasphemies and heresies should be suppressed, all corruptions and abuses in worship and discipline prevented or reformed." The Confession quotes various verses in Deuteronomy 13 dealing with idolatry.

23. John Calvin and William Pringle, *Commentary on a Harmony of the Evangelists Matthew, Mark, and Luke, vol. 1* (Bellingham, WA: Logos Bible Software, 2010), 447.

24. "Houses" in the Hebrew culture were often more than just a single nuclear family. They often included extended family and servants.

25. Nehemiah's social confession while under Persian rule is a good example (Neh. 8-10).

26. Rushdoony comments on this passage and notes that while this passage calls for the death penalty for idolatry, it does not call for the death penalty for unbelief and heresy. Rather, it is condemning to death any city that establishes another religion. He goes on to say that this condemnation does not apply to a missionary situation. Idolatry is treason in a sense. If a country has not established a covenant with God, they would not be guilty of treason. I agree with his position. The difficulty for us is whether or not we have committed treason. I believe most likely we have because our country, though it did not confess Christ openly as it should have in our constitution, did have a Christian heritage. In other words, not only are we guilty of the general revelation revealing the glory of God, but we are guilty because we had the special revelation law-word and turned away. Thus I think Rushdoony is right about the missionary exemption, but we can't really claim it the way, say, a city in North Korea could. Also see Matthew 11:20-21 for the concept that if a city is presented with the gospel and refuses it, it is cursed. Rushdoony, *The Institutes of Biblical Law, vol. 1*, 38-39.

27. Deuteronomy 21:1-9 and Numbers 35:2 also show the connection between the town and the surrounding countryside.

28. Joshua 15 lays out the concept that villages belong to cities. Here we see eleven districts created and identified with and by their central towns. The geography of these regions is contiguous, so the country between them must be included. See Roland de Vaux, *Ancient Israel* (New York: McGraw-Hill, 1961), 135.

29. Two other examples are the Rechabites (Jer. 35:14-19) and Obed-Edom (2 Sam. 6:12). I believe that these show God's willingness to

bless families in cursed areas, but they are still living in the midst of cursed societies. We should be thankful for this, but we should also realize this is presented in the Bible as a long-term strategy. The Lord wants nations, not just families. See chapter eight for more on this topic.

30. Also, the fact that Jesus showed us a house can be cursed means that a house can be blessed (Matt. 10:14-15).

31. Leviticus 26:44 tells us that even though God's people are caught up in judgment, He will not utterly destroy them.

32. God may provide short-term protection for His people in the midst of an ungodly society. Psalms has much to say about God protecting the righteous. However, these protections are not the same as the long-term, generational and societal blessings we see in Deuteronomy 28. Another example is the Israelites in Egypt and Babylon. God protected His people in the midst of a cursed people and land. It's important to point out, however, that Israel was allowed to leave these areas and therefore get out from the long-term curses.

33. *Westminster Confession of Faith* (Free Presbyterian Church of Scotland, 1976), 363.

4. CHRIST'S MEDIATORIAL REIGN

1. What about when Jesus said, "My kingdom is not of this world" (John 18:36)? The Greek word for "of" here is εκ ("ek"). It means "from," denoting origin. Jesus is saying His Kingdom does not originate from the world; otherwise those people who made Him king would be fighting for Him. He is not denying earthy authority at all.

2. Smith, *God and Politics*, 178.

3. Smith, *God and Politics*, 178.

4. Smith, *God and Politics*, 178.

5. See Chapter 7 for more examples of the new covenant requirement for civil magistrates to confess Christ.

6. William Symington and Raymond Patton Joseph, *Messiah the Prince* (Pittsburgh: Christian Statesman Press, 1999), 5.

7. DeMar, *God and Government*, xi.

8. Calvin, *Commentary on the Book of the Prophet Isaiah, vol. 1*, 91.

9. See Phillip G. Kayser, "When Do the Last Days Begin?" June 23, 2018, accessed December, 2020, https://kaysercommentary.com/Blogs/Last%20Days%20BeginBC.md.

10. John Gill, *An Exposition of the Old Testament, vol. 5*, The Baptist Commentary Series (London: Mathews and Leigh, 1810), 12.

11. See Phillip G. Kayser, "New Heaven and New Earth," November 9, 2018, accessed December, 2021, https://kaysercommentary.com/Sermons/New%20Testament/Revelation/Revelation%2021/Revelation%2021-1.md.
12. "And they that use this world, as not abusing it: for the fashion of this world passeth away. But I would have you without carefulness. He that is unmarried careth for the things that belong to the Lord, how he may please the Lord" (1 Cor. 7:31-32).
13. 13 Augustine, *The City of God* (New York: Random House, 1950), 732. Quoted by Phil Kayser in the above sermon preached on November 9, 2018.
14. Deuteronomy 30:11-15 warns against the idea that heaven's ethics are out of reach. Romans 10:5-8 repeats this warning.
15. Kayser, "New Heaven and New Earth," https://kaysercommentary.com/Sermons/New%20Testament/Revelation/Revelation%2021/Revelation%2021-1.md.
16. David M. Carson article in Smith, *God and Politics*, 120.

5. COMPREHENSIVENESS REQUIRED TODAY

1. Abraham Kuyper, *Lectures on Calvinism* (Grand Rapids: Eerdmans, 1987), 33.
2. Kuyper, *Lectures on Calvinism*, 23.
3. For example, Kuyper thought that Christian schools were the best way to train young children in righteousness. If he were alive today, one wonders if he would instead put homeschooling first.
4. At his inauguration speech at the Free University of Amsterdam, Kuyper said, "there is not one square inch in the whole domain of our human life of which Christ, who is Sovereign over all, does not cry, 'Mine!'" Abraham Kuyper, "Sphere Sovereignty: A public address delivered at the inauguration of the Free University, Oct. 20, 1880," accessed November, 2020, http://www.reformationalpublishingproject.com/pdf_books/Scanned_Books_PDF/SphereSovereignty_English.pdf.
5. Westminster Confession of Faith 23.3.
6. Also see Romans 13:1, 4.
7. William Henry Foote, *The Huguenots; or, Reformed French Church* (Harrisonburg: Sprinkle Publications, 2002), 3.
8. Foote, *The Huguenots*, 4.
9. Dietrich Bonhoeffer, *Life Together* (San Fransisco: Harper Collins, 1978), 18. For example, Bonhoeffer seems to present the idea that Christians being scattered is a good thing. He writes, "According to

God's will, Christendom is a scattered people." Strangely, the verse he uses to support this position is Deuteronomy 28:25: "The LORD shall cause thee to be smitten before thine enemies: thou shalt go out one way against them, and flee seven ways before them: and shalt be removed into all the kingdoms of the earth."

10. Romans 9:5-6 differentiates between Israel as the physical descendants of Abraham and the true, spiritual descendants.

11. Alan Heimert and Andrew Delbanco, eds., *The Puritans in America: A Narrative Anthology* (Cambridge, Mass.: Harvard University Press, 1985), 127. Taken from Joel R. Beeke and Mark Jones, *A Puritan Theology: Doctrine for Life* (Grand Rapids: Reformation Heritage Books, 2012), 773.

12. See Joshua 24:14. At the end of Joshua's life, he says, "ye know in all your hearts and in all your souls, that not one thing hath failed of all the good things which the LORD your God spake concerning you; all are come to pass unto you, and not one thing hath failed thereof" (Josh. 23:14).

13. Jon Acuff, *Finish: Give Yourself the Gift of Done* (New York: Penguin, 2017), 8.

14. Cornelius Van Til, *The Defense of the Faith* (P & R Publishing, 2008), 276.

15. R. J. Rushdoony, *This Independent Republic* (Vallecito: Chalcedon Foundation, 2001), xiv.

6. SOCIAL CONFESSIONALISM

1. Scott, *Distinctive Principles of the Reformed Presbyterian Church*, 26.

2. Heather Clark, "Mayor of Ashland, Ohio Dedicates City to Jesus Christ: 'May This Be a Land Where He Rules Supreme,'" Christian News Network, September 2, 2020, accessed October, 2020, https://christiannews.net/2020/09/02/mayor-of-ashland-ohio-dedicates-city-to-jesus-christ-may-this-be-a-land-where-he-rules-supreme/.

3. We can also say there are four governments: the individual (self-government) plus the three societal governments (family, church, and civil magistrate).

4. Greg L. Bahnsen, *Theonomy in Christian Ethics* (Nacogdoches: Covenant Media Press, 2002), 517.

5. John Gill, An Exposition of the Old Testament, vol. 1, The Baptist Commentary Series (London: Mathews and Leigh, 1810), 422-423.

6. Moses intermediated the covenant arrangement. Today, we still have a mediator, the man Jesus Christ (1 Tim. 2:5). He is the One to whom and by whom social confessions are made.

7. 7 Haggai 1:12-13 is another example of social confession in monumental times, in this case to build the temple.
8. *Westminster Confession of Faith*, 364.

7. NATIONAL CONFESSIONALISM, MODIFIED FOR COUNTY

1. William Einwechter, ed., *Explicitly Christian Politics* (Pittsburg, PA: The Christian Statesman Press, 2001), 88. William Edgar writing
2. Einwechter, *Explicitly Christian Politics*, 3, quoting David McAllister, *Christian Civil Government in America*, rev. by T. H. Acheson and Wm. Parsons, 6th ed. (Pittsburgh: National Reform Association, 1927), 20-21.
3. Einwechter, *Explicitly Christian Politics*, 5, quoting McAllister, *Christian Civil Government*.
4. Paul gets another appearance by the Lord in Acts 23:11 that seems to be another fulfillment of this calling: "And the night following the Lord stood by him, and said, Be of good cheer, Paul: for as thou hast testified of me in Jerusalem, so must thou bear witness also at Rome."
5. Smith, *God and Politics*, William Edgar writing. 173.
6. Symington and Joseph, *Messiah the Prince*, xi.
7. Smith, *God and Politics*, William Edgar writing, 173.
8. Symington and Joseph, *Messiah the Prince*, 189.
9. Smith, *God and Politics*, 180.
10. As we have stated before, the Bible uses "nations" for small as well as large societies with a legal, social structure.

8. OTHER SOCIETAL APPROACHES

1. Westminster Shorter Catechism Question 7. "Q: What are the decrees of God? A: The decrees of God are, his eternal purpose, according to the counsel of his will, whereby, for his own glory, he hath foreordained whatsoever comes to pass."
2. Westminster Confession of Faith 14.1.
3. John Calvin and Charles William Bingham, *Commentaries on the Four Last Books of Moses Arranged in the Form of a Harmony, vol. 3* (Bellingham, WA: Logos Bible Software, 2010), 220.
4. While the Bible does show that societal sins still require a separate, societal confession, there is overlap between the two. If someone commits the crime that caused societal guilt, he is personally guilty. And if someone is complacent, he bears the guilt. Calvin is not

comfortable with this distinction between temporal and eternal sins, nor is Francis Turretin. I can see the point because Leviticus 26 which we have been using for social confession does indeed have language which indicates that this is the same as personal confession: "if then their uncircumcised hearts be humbled" (Lev. 26:41). Perhaps if we look at curses in terms of punishment, that will help. The Lord will punish those He loves (Heb. 12:6). And this punishment can lead to repentance, which can lead to blessing instead of punishment on earth. Joshua, who was a man of God, went from being accursed by Achan's sin on earth to being blessed by God on earth (Josh. 7:12).

5. I disagree with Calvin on this point. He says the eternal-temporal distinction is not correct. Calvin holds that a father's sin causes God to withdraw His gracious hand from the father to some extent. That causes the sons to become more sinful and therefore pile more condemnation on themselves. My view is that there is a temporal-eternal distinction present throughout the Bible: earthly ramifications remain even with heavenly forgiveness. Punishment for murder is one example. Calvin, *Institutes*, 2.8.19-20. Turretin agrees with Calvin. Francis Turretin, *Institutes of Elenctic Theology, vol. 1* (Phillipsburg: P & R Publishing Company, 1997), 620-624.

6. There are still repercussions for a father's sin to the third and fourth generation. It is still a good idea to confess the sins of your ancestors to the third and fourth generation (Ex. 34:7) to remove any legal claim these curses may have on you or your family personally. See Robert Fugate's *Biblical Curses: Divine and Demonic*.

7. By "eternal" here I mean all of time. When we are forgiven in Christ, all our sins are forgiven, past, present, and future.

8. Isaiah 43:1-3 says that to be called by the name of God means that He is that person or society's Savior: "But now thus saith the LORD that created thee, O Jacob, and he that formed thee, O Israel, Fear not: for I have redeemed thee, I have called thee by thy name; thou art mine. When thou passest through the waters, I will be with thee; and through the rivers, they shall not overflow thee: when thou walkest through the fire, thou shalt not be burned; neither shall the flame kindle upon thee. For I am the LORD thy God, the Holy One of Israel, thy Saviour: I gave Egypt for thy ransom, Ethiopia and Seba for thee."

9. Some would disagree and say we do have a national covenant. Some say the Mayflower Compact is our covenant. Others, such as Gary DeMar, believe our constitution is Christian. *Smith, God and Politics, 200-212.*

10. We also need to be careful that we accept God's punishment rather than ignore it or say that we are not guilty of national sins: "and they

then accept the punishment of their iniquity" (Lev. 26:41).

11. Gary North, *Restoration and Dominion: An Economic Commentary on the Prophets* (Dallas: Point Five Press, 2012), 6.

12. Especially since we are sealed by the Holy Spirit (Eph. 1:13).

13. Another example of preservation by geographical separation comes to us in the example of the two baskets of figs in Jeremiah 24. The basket of good figs (v. 1) receives blessings and a promise of return (vv. 5-7), and the basket of bad figs stays in the land (v. 8), and God will deliver them to other nations, and they will receive pestilence and famine (vv. 9-10).

14. "Not utterly" is used often in the Bible. It means that we will survive and continue generationally, but we will not necessarily thrive.

15. It seems in Jeremiah 5:1 that just one righteous man would prevent judgment, but later we read that God does not even want Jeremiah to pray for the city because it's too far gone: "Therefore pray not thou for this people, neither lift up cry nor prayer for them, neither make intercession to me: for I will not hear thee" (Jer. 7:16). This is repeated in Jeremiah 14:11 and 15:1. Jeremiah 29:7 is a place where the church can pray for the peace of city while in captivity, but the primary beneficiary of the peace is not the city but Israel. In other words, this intercessory prayer is not really interceding on behalf of Babylon.

16. For example, the remnant of Israel was to preserve a line for the coming new covenant. See G. K. Beale, *A New Testament Biblical Theology: The Unfolding of the Old Testament in the New* (Baker Academic, 2011), 732.

17. Of course there is no problem with self-defense. We have a duty to be prepared (Ex. 22:2-3; Luke 11:21).

18. Deuteronomy 9:19 and Psalm 106:23 show that Moses' intercession allowed the nation to continue but did not secure forgiveness.

19. See also Deuteronomy 9:18-26. Here Moses is recounting the fact that he interceded and God did not destroy the line of Israel.

20. Moses prays a similar prayer in Numbers 14:11-20. God answers (v. 20) and says He forgives, but this is only temporary forgiveness (v. 23).

21. Intercessory prayer may find forgiveness if a covenantal head prays within his own jurisdiction. Job confesses the sins of his family and seems to have found forgiveness for those sins (Job 1:5). I take this to mean family-based sins.

22. Samuel is important because he shows that church leaders and members should pray for society. The church can't expect God to forgive the nation based on their prayers (Ezek. 14:14), but they can secure mercy to enable time for repentance, and they can pray (like Samuel did) that the people will repent. Samuel later, as a spirit,

rejects Saul's plea to pray for him because Saul had not repented (1 Sam. 15:24-26).

23. Another example with Samuel is in 1 Samuel 8:5-10. Here again, however, it was a public assembly (vv. 4-6), and Samuel was praying as a representative.

24. Keith A. Mathison, *Postmillennialism: An Eschatology of Hope* (P & R Publishing, 1999), 221.

25. Ezra also invokes the idea of a remnant (Ezra 9:8) as a result of intercessory prayer.

26. Christ has the legal union necessary to enable Him to interpose on our behalf. "Substitution is only possible when the guilt can be transferred from the sinner and imputed to the substitute because of a legal union between them (2 Cor. 5:21; Phil. 3:9)." Joel R. Beeke, Michael P. V. Barrett, and Gerald M. Bilkes, eds., *The Reformation Heritage KJV Study Bible* (Grand Rapids, MI: Reformation Heritage Books, 2014). See remarks on v. 32:33. Also see point 2 under "Thoughts for Persona/Family Worship, 136.

9. CONFESSIONAL COUNTY STRATEGY

1. The term "nations" is used in the Bible of both small and large societies, geophysically located, with a regency (Acts 13:19).

2. Beale, *A New Testament Biblical Theology: The Unfolding of the Old Testament in the New*, 340.

3. North, *Political Polytheism*, xviii, quoting Lewis in C. S. Lewis, *That Hideous Strength* (New York: Macmillan, 1946), 283.

4. Quoted in William S. Barker and Samuel T. Logan Jr., eds., *Sermons That Shaped America* (Phillipsburg, N.J.: P&R, 2003), 35-36. Extracted from Beeke and Jones, *A Puritan Theology: Doctrine for Life*, 773.

5. With the exception of cyber. It is very difficult to leapfrog with this one because worldwide development happens so quickly. You don't really have time to ignore the enemy like you could with nukes.

10. CULTURE, BEAUTY AND WORSHIP AS A "WAY"

1. C. S. Lewis, *The Weight of Glory* (New York: Harper Collins, 2001), 26.

2. James K. A. Smith, *You Are What You Love* (Brazos Press, 2016), 57.

3. Smith, *You Are What You Love*, 12.

4. Cotton Mather, *Magnalia Christi Americana: or, the Ecclesiastical History of New-England, vol. 1* (Hartford: Roberts & Burr, 1820), 46.

5. Foote, *The Huguenots,*, 11.
6. Foote, *The Huguenots*, 185.
7. Foote, *The Huguenots*, 185.
8. Geoffrey Treasure, *The Huguenots* (New Haven: Yale University Press, 2013), 109.
9. Foote, *The Huguenots*, 11.
10. Douglas Jones and Douglas Wilson, *Angels in the Architecture: A Protestant Vision for Middle Earth* (Canon Press, 1998), 174.
11. Jones and Wilson, *Angels in the Architecture*, 179.
12. The term "Luddism" today generally refers to someone opposed to technology.
13. Mervin Breneman, *Ezra, Nehemiah, Esther, vol. 10,* electronic ed., The New American Commentary (Nashville: Broadman & Holman Publishers, 1993), 91.
14. Carl von Clausewitz, *On War* (Princeton: Princeton Press, 1976), 254-255.
15. John Calvin, *Institutes of the Christian Religion,* 4.18.16.
16. "Therefore if any man be in Christ, he is a new creature: old things are passed away; behold, all things are become new" (2 Cor. 5:17).

11. LOCALISM AS A "WAY"

1. Thomas L. Friedman, *The World is Flat* (New York: Macmillan, 2005), 51.
2. Friedman, *The World is Flat*, 159-172.
3. R. J. Rushdoony, "The Theology of the Land," Rushdoony Radio, https://rushdoonyradio.org/theology-of-the-land/.
4. Here we do not have heads of families as in Nehemiah's confession, but the elders are certainly fathers as well, so they are probably wearing two hats.
5. Vaux, *Ancient Israel*, 78.
6. Even large cities were interconnected. During the siege of Jerusalem, Josephus said there were 2.7 million at the feast of unleavened bread just before the city was besieged, and 1.1 million were killed. Most of these did not belong to the city itself. But you can see the interconnectedness of Jerusalem during the same feast just forty years before, where all Jerusalem was in an uproar. Josephus, *The Wars of the Jews*, Book VI Ch 9 Sec 3.
7. Rushdoony, "The Theology of the Land," https://rushdoonyradio.org/theology-of-the-land/.
8. This condemnation applies to cities that have heard the gospel and subsequently rejected it as a city (Deut. 13:12-18; Matt. 11:20-21).

9. In Luke 14:28-30, Jesus tells us to count the cost of building. I realize this passage is talking about counting the cost of following Jesus, and the main point is to forsake all, no matter the cost. My point is that there is a principle that makes Jesus' point possible, that some things take longer than others, even though (and perhaps because) we are walking with the Spirit in our daily battles. Sometimes I think we under-analyze if we only ask the question, "Can't God save New York City?" We need to consider not just God's capability but also consider how He works in history. The mustard seed grows slowly. The question, I think, for fathers today is similar to the question of fathers in Leyden in 1620. Can we hold back culture long enough to change it before it captures our children?

10. Rushdoony says heresy and unbelief do not constitute the public idolatry that causes a city to be cursed. It is rather cities that "establish" another religion. By "establish," I take it that he means religion publicly exercised and allowed (and even encouraged). Rushdoony, *The Institutes of Biblical Law, vol. 1*, 39.

11. Jones and Wilson, *Angels in the Architecture*, 132.

12. Jones and Wilson, *Angels in the Architecture*, 143.

13. Trewhella, *Doctrine of the Lesser Magistrates*, 41.

14. Trewhella,, *The Doctrine of the Lesser Magistrates*, 18.

15. Samuel Rutherford, *Lex Rex, or the Law and the Prince* (Harrisonburg: Sprinkle Publications, 1982), 54.

16. Trewhella, *The Doctrine of the Lesser Magistrates*, 31-37.

17. Colin Woodard, *American Nations: A History of the Eleven Rival Regional Cultures of North America*, (New York: Penguin, 2011), 317.

18. Tom Pappert, "UPDATE: 21 States Now Support Texas SCOTUS Lawsuit, 42% of America to Sue 8% of America," National File, December 10, 2020, accessed March, 2021, https://nationalfile.com/update-21-states-now-support-texas-scotus-lawsuit-42-of-america-to-sue-8-of-america/.

19. Personal conversation with Paul Michael Raymond. February, 2021.

20. Erin O'Donnell, "The Risks of Homeschooling," *Harvard Magazine*, May-June 2020, accessed March, 2021, https://harvardmagazine.com/2020/05/right-now-risks-homeschooling.

12. REVIVING THE CHRISTIAN SETTLEMENT

1. Rushdoony, *This Independent Republic*, 48.

2. Also, America's quest for political liberty, developed in the First Great Awakening, may have contributed to the end of colonialism.

See Vishal Mangalwadi, *The Book That Changed Your World* (Nashville: Thomas Nelson, 2011), 380.

3. Christopher Columbus, *Book of Prophecies,* quoted by Steven J. Wilkins, *America: The First 350 Years,* Lecture 2.
4. Mangalwadi, *The Book That Changed Your World,* 122.
5. Wilkins, *America: The First 350 Years,* Lecture 2.
6. John M. Frame, *Systematic Theology: An Introduction to Christian Belief,* (P & R Publishing, 2013), 63.
7. C. H. Spurgeon, "Canaan on Earth," a sermon preached on December 30, 1855, accessed January 2021, https://archive. spurgeon.org/sermons/0058.php.
8. Rushdoony, *This Independent Republic,* 43. I think one reason why this right had to be spelled out was because the mindset of that day was more covenantal. People felt obligated to their leaders and society. Today's American independent mind has a hard time grasping the concept of a covenanted church, much less a covenanted society.
9. Frame, *Systematic Theology,* 87.
10. Daniel J. Ford, *In the Name of God, Amen: Rediscovering Biblical and Historical Covenants* (St. Louis: Lex Rex Publishing, 2002), 152.
11. "One in Five Americans Live in Rural Areas," United States Census Bureau, August 9, 2017, accessed January 2021, https://www.census. gov/library/stories/2017/08/rural-america.html.
12. Contact https://cviog.uga.edu/local-government-resources-landing.html for information on how to do this.
13. "Kansas Counties by Population," Kansas Demographics, accessed January 2021, https://www.kansas-demographics.com/counties_by_population.
14. It is also important to see the limits of the Federal government here. They could not mandate local policy during the Pandemic; only governors could do that.
15. Sumner Chilton Powell, *Puritan Village: The Formation of a New England Town* (Hanover: Wesleyan University Press, 1963), 5.

13. UTOPIA?

1. Bonhoeffer, *Life Together,* 28.
2. Walter A. Elwell, *Evangelical Dictionary of Theology* (Grand Rapids: Baker, 2001), 1235.
3. Elwell, *Evangelical Dictionary of Theology,* 1236.
4. John M. Frame, *A History of Western Philosophy and Theology* (P & R Publishing, 2015), 285.
5. Gordon Clark, *Thales to Dewey* (Trinity Foundation, 2000), 240.
6. Joseph Boot, *The Mission of God* (London: Wilberforce, 2016), 159.

7. Boot, *The Mission of God*, 160.
8. Boot, *The Mission of God*, 163.
9. Psalm 96:9.

14. THE CONFESSIONAL COUNTY, PRACTICALLY

1. Home rule is a broader concept often applied to territories of nations. It makes them a self-governing nation even though owned by another country. The Faroe Islands of Denmark are a good example. The American City County Exchange has an excellent resource entitled "Federalism, Dillon Rule and Home Rule" (January 2016) available here: https://www.alec.org/app/uploads/2016/01/2016-ACCE-White-Paper-Dillon-House-Rule-Final.pdf.
2. The states that have Home Rule but not Dillon Rule are: AK, CT, IA, MI, MN, NV, PA, SC, TX, WI, WV.
3. Rushdoony writes, "Biblical law has no property tax; the right to tax real property is implicitly denied to the state, because the state has no earth to tax. 'The earth is the Lord's' (Ex. 9:29; Deut. 10:14; Ps. 24:1; I Cor. 10:26, etc.)." Rushdoony, *The Institutes of Biblical Law, vol. 1*, 56.
4. A homeschooling father and friend of mine owns two houses. He and his family live in one during the non-legislative session and the other during the session. While I commend him for not separating himself from his family, this is not a good situation to put ourselves in if we have a choice.
5. Contact BiblicalBlueprints for a copy at info@biblicalblueprints.com

15. CONCLUSION

1. Lewis, *Weight of Glory*, 54
2. Lewis, *Weight of Glory*, 54.
3. Outwardly speaking. Worship is primary as we are made primarily to worship God.

APPENDIX B: LOCATION CRITERIA

1. Home Rule means the county or municipality can make any laws that do not conflict with the state's laws. Dillon's Rule means counties and municipalities can only make laws the state specifically permits.

APPENDIX C: SAMPLE COUNTY CONFESSION

1. Section taken and modified from the Solemn League and Covenant of Scotland.
2. Section taken directly from the Magdeburg Confession, Kindle Edition. Translated by Matthew Colvina and published by Matthew Trewhella.
3. Taken directly from Raymond Simmons, *Dunedin Documents: A Vision & Plan for Local Christendom* (2019). Available by request at theconfessionalists.com.

APPENDIX D: WHAT YOU CAN DO AT THE COUNTY LEVEL

1. For the unborn, see https://personhood.org/safecity/
2. See https://sanctuarycounties.com/ for more information on sanctuary counties. Note: Google searches will not display sanctuary county information.
3. Rushdoony writes, "Biblical law has no property tax; the right to tax real property is implicitly denied to the state, because the state has no earth to tax. 'The earth is the Lord's' (Ex. 9:29; Dt. 10:14; Ps. 24:1; I Cor. 10:26, etc.)." Rushdoony, *The Institutes of Biblical Law, vol. 1*, 56.
   Also see Robert Fugate, *Toward a Theology of Taxation* (Omaha: Lord of the Nations, 2012), 48-67; and Robert Fugate, "The Head Tax: the Only God-Endorsed Civil Tax," *Faith for All of Life*, July/August 2012, accessed March, 2021, https://chalcedon.edu/magazine/the-head-tax-the-only-god-endorsed-civil-tax.

BIBLIOGRAPHY

Acuff, Jon. *Finish*. New York: Penguin, 2017.

Augustine. *The City of God*. New York: Random House, Modern Library, 1950.

Bahnsen, Greg L. *Theonomy in Christian Ethics*. Nacogdoches: Covenant Media Press, 2002.

Beale, G. K. *A New Testament Biblical Theology: The Unfolding of the Old Testament in the New*. Baker Academic, 2011.

Beeke, Joel R., and Mark Jones. *A Puritan Theology: Doctrine for Life*. Grand Rapids: Reformation Heritage Books, 2012.

Bonhoeffer, Dietrich. *Life Together*. San Francisco: Harper Collins, 1978.

Boot, Joseph. *The Mission of God*. London: Wilberforce, 2016.

Bradford, William. *Of Plymouth Plantation, 1620-1647*. New York: Rutgers University Press, 1952.

Calvin, John. *Institutes of the Christian Religion*. Edited by John T. McNeill; translated by Ford Lewis Battles. Philadelphia: Westminster Press, 1961.

Clark, Gordon. *Thales to Dewey*. Trinity Foundation, 2000.

von Clausewitz, Carl. *On War*. Michael Howard and Peter Paret, eds. Princeton: Princeton Press, 1976.

Dabney, Robert Lewis. *Life and Campaigns of Lieutenant General Thomas J. Stonewall Jackson*. Harrisonburg: Sprinkle Publications, 1983.

DeMar, Gary. *God and Government*. Powder Springs, Georgia: American Vision, 2011.

Dreher, Rod. *The Benedict Option: A Strategy for Christians in a Post-Christian Nation*. New York: Penguin, 2017.

Einwechter, William O. *Explicitly Christian Politics*. Edited by William O. Einwechter. Pittsburg, PA: The Christian Statesman Press, 2001.

Elwell, Walter A. *Evangelical Dictionary of Theology*. Grand Rapids: Baker Academic, 2001.

Foote, William Henry. *The Huguenots; or, Reformed French Church.* Harrisonburg: Sprinkle Publications, 2002.

Ford, Daniel J. *In the Name of God, Amen: Rediscovering Biblical and Historical Covenants.* St. Louis: Lex Rex Publishing, 2002.

Frame, John M. *Systematic Theology: An Introduction to Christian Belief.* P & R Publishing, 2013.

———. *A History of Western Philosophy and Theology.* P & R Publishing, 2015.

Friedman, Thomas L. *The World is Flat.* New York: Macmillan, 2005.

Fugate, Robert. *Toward a Theology of Taxation.* Omaha: Lord of the Nations, 2012.

Grimstead, Jay, and Eugene Clingman. *Rebuilding Civilization on the Bible.* Ventura: Nordskog, 2014.

Jones, Douglas, and Douglas Wilson. *Angels in the Architecture: A Protestant Vision for Middle Earth.* Canon Press, 1998.

Kurland, Philip B., and Ralph Lerner. *The Founders' Constitution.* 1987.

Kuyper, Abraham. *Lectures on Calvinism.* 8th ed. Grand Rapids: Eerdmans, 1987.

Lewis, C. S. *The Weight of Glory.* New York: Harper Collins, 2001.

Makers of Modern Strategy: From Machiavelli to the Nuclear Age. Edited by Peter Paret. Princeton: Princeton Press, 1986.

Mangalwadi, Vishal. *The Book That Changed Your World.* Nashville: Thomas Nelson, 2011.

Mathison, Keith A. *Postmillennialism: An Eschatology of Hope.* P & R Publishing, 1999.

Morecraft, Joseph C. *Authentic Christianity: An Exposition of the Theology and the Ethics of the Westminster Larger Catechism (5 volumes).* American Vision, 2009.

North, Gary. *Political Polytheism: The Myth of Pluralism.* Tyler: Institute for Christian Economics, 1989.

———. *Restoration and Dominion: An Economic Commentary on the Prophets.* Dallas: Point Five Press, 2012.

Powell, Sumner Chilton. *Puritan Village: The Formation of a New England Town.* Hanover: Wesleyan University Press, 1963.

Rushdoony, R. J. *This Independent Republic.* Vallecito: Chalcedon Foundation, 2001.

———. *The Institutes of Biblical Law (three volumes).* P & R Publishing Co., 1973.

Rutherford, Samuel. *Lex Rex, or the Law and the Prince.* Harrisonburg: Sprinkle Publications, 1982.

Sandlin, P. Andrew. *Religion Realized.* Coulterville: Center for Cultural Leadership, 2021.

Scott, David. *Distinctive Principles of the Reformed Presbyterian Church.* Albany: Munsell, 1841.

Smith, Gary Scott. *God and Politics.* P & R Publishing Company, 1989.

Smith, James K. A. *You Are What You Love.* Brazos Press, 2016.

Solberg, Winton U. *Redeem the Time: The Puritan Sabbath in Early America.* Harvard University Press, 1977.

Symington, William, and Raymond Patton Joseph. *Messiah the Prince.* Pittsburgh: Christian Statesman Press, 1999.

Treasure, Geoffrey. *The Huguenots.* New Haven: Yale University Press, 2013.

Trewhella, Matthew J. *The Doctrine of the Lesser Magistrates: A Proper Resistance to Tyranny and a Repudiation of Unlimited Obedience to Civil Government.* North Charleston: CreateSpace Independent Publishing Platform, 2013.

Turretin, Francis. *Institutes of Elenctic Theology (three volumes).* Phillipsburg: P & R Publishing Company, 1997.

Van Til, Cornelius. *The Defense of the Faith.* Edited by K. Scott Oliphint. P & R Publishing, 2008.

Vaux, Roland de. *Ancient Israel.* New York: McGraw-Hill, 1961.

Veith Jr., Gene Edward. *Post-Christian.* Crossway Books, 2020.

Westminster Confession of Faith. Free Presbyterian Church of Scotland, 1976.

Woodard, Colin. *American Nations: A History of the Eleven Rival Regional Cultures of North America*. New York: Penguin, 2011.

ABOUT THE AUTHOR

Lt. Col. (Ret.) Raymond Simmons graduated from Texas
Tech University before becoming a pilot in the Air Force.
As a staff officer, he led the planning for USSTRATCOM's
Strategic Deterrence Campaign Plan. He also served as
international relations advisor to Admiral Haney.

Since retiring from the Air Force, Ray teaches part-time
at Air University. In 2020, he became a Senior Executive
Fellow at Harvard's Kennedy School of Government.

He has been blessed to study under Phil Kayser (PhD),
president of Biblical Blueprints and instructor at White-
field Theological Seminary.

Ray lives with his wife and eight children in a 100-year-
old colonial home in a beautiful Midwest town. He enjoys
homeschooling his eight children and feasting with the
church body.

Made in the USA
Monee, IL
25 May 2022

97024062R00152